ISBN: 9798772035405

Front & back cover designed by Badja O'Connell.

Printed by Amazon Inc., in the United Kingdom

First printing edition 2021.

Facebook Group: We're all about Poodles.

This book is dedicated to
Daisy,

Ruler of the universe

Tales From Poodle Central

Part 3

"The End of an Era"

Part 4

"Who's Randy Rooster?"

Written By

Simone Parkinson

Editor-In-Chief

Andrea Mills

Front & Back Cover Design

Badja O'Connell.

Welcome!

I hope you enjoyed reading the first parts of our journey and tales

You join us as our family had welcomed the arrival of Lupin - everything will go smoothly, right?

Well as we know poodle wrangling is never predictable so read on in part three "The End of an Era"

Then read the continued Tales from Poodle Central part four "Who's Randy Rooster?" the daily antics of the Little Parkinson's

It's never quiet... but it's always fun

Simone x

Part 3

The End Of An Era

CHAPTER 1

You left us at Poodle Central with Lupin arriving early November and 3 birthdays on the horizon

It was all go!

Restrictions due to the covid virus meant not all shops were open and to pull off 3 birthday celebrations we had to get creative

26th November Daisy was celebrating her 17th birthday, 28th November Lupin was turning 1 and 30th November Alfie was reaching 14!

Balloons were ordered, cakes were ordered,

But it was hard as the grief we felt losing Belle was still at the forefront, but we also knew we couldn't let birthdays pass without celebrating

I'd ordered the balloons locally and I had to collect them on the day, I smiled because the owner of the shop said to me "you've a spread-out family"

"Yes, I chuckled"

So, Daisy's birthday arrived and my little girl turned 17!

In typical Daisy style she marched past her balloons and went straight to the treats safe in the knowledge her Kentucky chicken would

arrive later in the day

Cream cake number 1 was demolished and 3 happy poodles flopped on the sofa

Next came Lupin and she reached the number 1!

Lupin happily posed next to her balloon and thoroughly enjoyed the whole Hoo Har of the day In fact, Lupin was on a roll, she decided birthdays should be every day of the week

Daisy gobbled back her 2nd Kentucky

Lastly (by this time even Teddy was feeling cakey full) came Alfie and his big 14th birthday!

Yet again I dutifully drove and collected the balloons, the cake and came home to start a day of celebrations

Daisy was whooping at the prospect of her 3rd Kentucky of the week, however as it's always the choice of the birthday boy or girl to choose their birthday treat and Daisy was sadly disappointed....

Alfie will always choose a McDonald burger lol

We'd reached the end of November with 3 happy poodles and a gaggle of helium balloons floating around the house

Proud poodle wranglers we were.

CHAPTER 2

As I've said before it's an over confident poodle wrangler who thinks they've seen it all, believe me for everything we see and experience these fur balls have plenty more to show!

So, imagine our surprise when we discovered Lupin went to sleep one night and woke up "the demon Lupin" the day after

The little girl had finished her season when she arrived at poodle central, and in all our years of poodle wrangling we'd never experienced "seasons" or gulp… "a phantom pregnancy"

Well fate was blowing us a raspberry and decided we needed a crash course - All squeaky toys became "babies" and Lupin would guard these with all her might …

On one occasion Daisy was just strolling by and the hormone riddled Lupini dived at her and had her (Daisy's) head in her mouth!

Now I'll never forget that scream Daisy gave out and my heart broke at her shock and pain,

But as responsible poodle wranglers we knew something was off with Lupin and it wasn't her fault

Daisy did forgive Lupin

After two trips to the vets Lupin was diagnosed with a phantom pregnancy and ta! da! - Inexperienced poodle wranglers we were yet again

Drops had to be given daily and all "babies" removed ...the top of my fridge freezer was piled high with them lol

Eventually Lupins hormones started to flatten and Daisy, Alfie and Teddy could walk past Lupin without wearing protective gear

Poor Lupin rehomed and then forced through a phantom pregnancy and poor us! never ever do I want to see a phantom pregnancy ever again....

The tree was put up, decorated with the poodles' ornaments but despite the joy Lupin brought, the sadness that Belle wasn't with us was hard

Lupin put her Christmas ornament on the tree and started her tradition - Stockings were hung

And Aldi released its range of Christmas stuffed toys from its now super popular "Kevin the carrot" range

Now a quick background on Aldi's toys

They started as an advert on U.K. television at Christmas and became an overnight success, so much so each year a new range is released and each year a frenzy is caused by shoppers trying to secure the toys

So, this year Aldi added a hedgehog to the Kevin the carrot family, now everyone who knows Teddy or read about him knows his favourite toys of all time are his hedgehogs

He loves them!

So, I promised him one, thinking I'd go and queue and get him one to unwrap on Christmas Day

However, the hedgehog sold out online in minutes! And I was seriously worried I'd disappoint him

But what I didn't reckon on was the power of the poodle community

Far and wide, they came together to organise and mobilise to secure a hedgehog for Teddy

I'd posted on a social media site asking if anyone saw a hedgehog in their local store could they get it for me? We were overwhelmed

North, South, East and West

Liverpool, Ireland, Formby, Birmingham, Morecambe

They rallied

Europe

They rallied

A good friend even went to her local Aldi looking for a hedgehog, even though she hates going into supermarkets

Teddy's hedgehog dream came true

In fact, his Christmas Day was a hedgehog spectacular

The poodle community sent him numerous hedgehogs and each one is loved

So, Christmas 2020 although tinged with sadness, also saw yet again the great heart the poodle community has....

CHAPTER 3

Entering 2021 we all breathed a sigh of relief to put 2020 behind us - 2020 had eaten us up, spit us out and still demanded more

All of us had suffered on all levels, just to be rid of 2020 we hoped for a better future, A future which would resemble our old normal

Here at poodle central our greatest wish was to be able to book our annual "poodles' holiday" and actually go!

January was spent dreaming of Lincolnshire beaches

It would be Lupins first trip to the seaside and her big reveal in person to some of our poodle friends

Excitement was building, however before all this Lupin had a date with the vets ...Yep, she was being spayed

Of course, we didn't tell Lupin this as she might have tried hightailing it to her Auntie Sues and renaming herself Doris!

So, the big day arrived and with covid restrictions still in place, it meant only one of us could go inside with her, now Lupin isn't daft as soon as I took her inside her inbuilt "vet Dar" went off and Lupin became the Lupini "I'm going back to my dad!"

Holding the now wriggling Lupin, we saw the vet and I told Lupin to be a good girl and I'd see her later

As many of you know, dropping off our fur balls is never easy- we worry, we telephone, and then we run as fast as we can as soon as we know we can pick them up

Lupin's spaying went well, her wound looked good

Lupin though looked like she'd been dragged through a hedge backwards ...

But she was home - Next was the Babygro....

Now I swear Daisy was laughing when we put Lupin's dinosaur Babygro on and I also swear the Lupini was dying from embarrassment but her "best friends" Babygro went on and it did the job And Lupin ticked being spayed off her bucket list - The early months passed by and hope was bright...

However, an emergency was waiting!

CHAPTER 4

We woke up one morning and everything seemed the norm, however when breakfast came Lupin didn't eat her breakfast with any gusto

In fact, she was particularly disinterested

This in itself was unusual for Lupin and my poogy sense started a tingling!

During the day she was very quiet and when Neil arrived home and she refused her tea (dinner) I was getting worried

She didn't seem to be able to settle

Daisy, Alfie and Teddy had been fine throughout the day and none of them could get a response out of Lupin

I telephoned the vets, I explained what was happening with Lupin and I said she wasn't drinking much either

They made us an appointment for the day after

When I took Lupin the morning after she still wasn't right and the vets decided she was dehydrated so it would be best to keep her in

Reluctantly I said yes- as we know it's hard to leave them, Lupin was not a happy camper

The vets telephoned the day after and they had performed various tests but could not pin point Lupin's problem so it was decided she could be discharged with some medication

Off we went to collect a very dishevelled Lupin, her poor hair had been shaved in spots all over and our little girl was now sporting one bald leg with a pom on it - But we were just glad she was home

However, things didn't go to plan, Lupin did not pick up and she still seemed lethargic

Ok I said give me the phone

I telephoned the vets and off we set again out of hours to take the poorly Lupin back

They kept her in again

However, this time when running the x rays and scans she tested positive for pancreatitis!

Oh my! Lupin was determined to make her mark but at least now we knew what we were dealing with

The vets kept Lupin in hospital for nearly 3 days and it was a very quiet time at poodle central, even Daisy was looking where the Lupini was, so when the vets said it would be ok for Lupin to come home a sigh of relief was breathed

Now this time when we picked Lupin up, well she looked like she'd been dragged through a hedge backwards with more creative shaving, her other front leg was shaved bald with a small pom on the bottom! Oh, poor Lupin

Well, we got her home and this time with the correct meds she rallied and got better

However, that left us with the quandary with what to do with her rather creative grooming

CHAPTER 5

We decided to break tradition at poodle central and Lupin went into a Miami type cut

She had a close shaved body - her now leg poms and fluffy tail and top knot, and it suited her!

Great job Tracy!

The sun was shining over poodle central and everything was looking good

Around this time the neighbours at the back of us decided to let their dog out more and we had the usual barky barky at the fence at the back of our garden, it became such a usual occurrence that two things happened

We started calling their dog the "rat" for no other reason than we couldn't think of a shortened name for a Shih tzu

And secondly Neil (after Teddy and Lupin trampled all my flowers near the fence) built the now known "rat run" which simply means he laid some flags / paving stones so that Teddy and Lupin could happily run along our side of the fence barking with the "rat"

The "rats" owner even comes out and claps his hands to announce its barky time.... life was good

However, during this time Daisy started to have little blips, she was restless at night, but in true Daisy fashion she bounced back

She was eating and drinking and along with Alfie, Teddy and Lupin thoroughly enjoying the artificial lawn we'd had laid earlier in the year

An explorers dream

However, one Saturday just before the second bank holiday things changed......

Daisy had partaken of her usual Saturday swimming and was sat on Neil's knee in the garden -I had just cleaned her potato ears and was commenting how she managed to get them waxy, I was met with the usual scowl

But when tea (dinner) was served and even my best rendition of "Hey Daisy Girl" (a play on the seekers Hey there Georgie Girl) failed to get Daisy to eat, my poogy sense started to tingle

Daisy was incredibly restless that night and even when I took her upstairs where it was quiet, she still couldn't settle

I walked the floor with her that night, holding her and trying to get her to have a drink, I knew how quickly dehydration could set in and I practically begged my little girl to have even a sip of water off my fingers

She eventually settled - Sunday morning, she still wasn't right and although we managed to get a little water into her, she had not eaten

We rang the vets, off I trotted with Daisy and I just naively presumed they would get some fluids into her and we'd be on our merry way

After all this was Daisy...My Daisy ruler of the universe

The vets kept Daisy in - And how I've run it through my mind should I have had her admitted??...would the chain of events altered???

Anyways the vets telephoned later that day and said they had found some sludge in Daisy's gall bladder but they had started treatment and she was bright

The vets wanted to keep her in overnight, I agreed

Later that evening I telephoned the vets and asked how my little girl was, they said she was settled but had still not eaten

I told them to telephone me for any minor change and the vet agreed as she told me she knew how much Daisy meant to me ...

The evening passed

And the next I heard was the telephone ringing at 7am Monday, the morning of the bank holiday.

CHAPTER 6

When I heard the phone ringing early Monday morning, I knew it was the vets

I presumed as I hadn't heard from them during the night all was well and Daisy was doing ok

How wrong could I be

The vet told me Daisy wasn't doing well, so much so they had moved her to an incubator to try and help her

My world was collapsing around me

I asked how she was now and I was told not good

During the night she had been very unwell and when I asked if this could be a reaction to the meds, they had started her on I was told no- the meds were supposed to help

My little girl □

We arranged for me to go and visit Daisy at 11am but when I put the phone down, I knew where I needed to be and got dressed to go be with my heart ❤□

When we arrived, we were told we should have telephoned first and I just looked at this vet debating whether I would strangle her now and waste time or save her for later.... I decided later

We were taken back to the hospital part where Daisy lay

My whole world shattered at that one moment and I cannot express the sheer sadness I felt

"Get her out if that now" I said to the nurses who watched as I ripped off my mask- there was no way I was loving my little girl behind a mask, I didn't give a rat's ass

They came and lifted Daisy into my arms and I felt her give a long sigh…. she knew I was there

"Mummy's here baby" I told her

"Get these tubes off her" I told the nurses

They removed the end of the drip and that's when I said I'm taking her outside

So, they opened the door and out I marched (it had to be a march after all I was with the ruler of the universe) into the bank holiday sun

I took her up to the top of the car park into the warm sun and broke my heart telling her I was sorry I couldn't do anymore but I wouldn't let her have pain or fight a fight she wasn't going to win

I told her Belle was waiting and it was her job to keep the snakeynapper in tow

I told my little girl I loved her from the first moment I set eyes on her in Neil's (her breeder) living room and I'll love her until time ends

I then took her back inside where the nurses where waiting and told them there was no way she was going back in that incubator

I had to clearly state what I wanted □

So, Me, Daisy and Neil went to the vet's calm room and again I told Daisy I promised her we would be together and she would never be on her own

Belle, Grandma and all her brothers and big sister were waiting to greet her and play

And with that my darling heart slipped away from me and this world and into the next

I truly felt fate was cruel - our baby Belle was taken just six months earlier and now Daisy too

I just had had enough

We walked out of the vets with the most precious bundle and tears were just falling

CHAPTER 7

As we walked out of the vets, my sister Sue arrivcd

I had telephoned to tell her how bad Daisy was and she rushed to the vets

I told her Daisy had passed ▢

The tears flowed for the loss of my little girl

We all went back home to the waiting Alfie, Teddy and Lupin

Daisy was placed on the sofa in her spot - comfy in a nest and blankie

Then all the gang made their way to her

This was all very new to Lupin and she didn't understand quite what was happening and why Daisy was still "asleep"

Teddy jumped up and snuggled her before jumping back down and retreating into his nest

As for Alfie, he took up position on the sofa next to Daisy and maintained guard

Only moving to eat, drink or pee pee

My total strength in this world had been taken, Daisy that teeny tiny dot had given me far far more than I could have ever thought

She was my heart

I knew I would have to put a post on Facebook for friends who had been concerned when Daisy took ill and the only post appropriate for the ruler of the universe was simply

"Scooby has Fallen"

Scooby was her nickname ❤️

Daisy had walked to the beat of her own drum for 17 1/2 years and I had been privileged to walk beside her

She had welcomed Alfie, Teddy, Belle and Lupin when they each arrived at poodle central

She was one of the last of her generation with her little docked tail

She was *"the ruler of the universe "*

As my world was falling apart, the outpouring of love for Daisy was overwhelming

I've said this before and I'll never tire of saying it the poodle community pulls together in times of need

And here at poodle central our need was great

We loved Alfie, Teddy and Lupin, we tried to help them cope with their loss but the grief I felt was profound

And then the messages started

The condolences

And then the flowers started to arrive

In their abundance

Yes, we had suffered another horrific loss so soon after Belle but we knew we weren't alone

CHAPTER 8

We buried Daisy adjacent to poodle mountain in a spot perfect for the ruler of the universe

Neil prepared the spot while we all watched solemnly, my heart aching at not only Daisy's passing but at the end of an era

For the 17 1/2 years that little ball had walked this earth I had happily walked beside her, now it was over

The messages and flowers we received certainly showed that small is mighty and that my little girl in her typical Daisy fashion had made her mark

A very good friend sent an outdoor wreath made up of daisy flowers and it now sits along with a guard of honour on Daisy's plot

Truly poodle central was being dragged through the wringer

Now as everyone knows by now Teddy is the thinker of the family and does things his way but Miss Lupin also left her mark with Daisy too

Teddy, shortly after we buried Daisy was found outside sitting on the grass next to Daisy's plot

Just sitting there - Just thinking

In typical Teddy style

But what I think surprised us was Lupin, she took her squeaky hedgehog (she adopted from Belle) and placed it in front of the guard on Daisy's plot

At first, I thought she'd accidentally dropped it and didn't know how to get it back so I went and picked it up and gave it back to Lupin

No

Lupin immediately took it back to Daisy, dropped it and walked away to play with something else

So, to all those folk out there in the world who say dogs have no feelings I say to you that you talk utter rubbish!

They do feel, they do grieve and in Teddy's and Lupins way they show their grief in their own way

I'll never have enough words to express my love and gratitude to friends who yet again rallied with us in our grief

Each message, each card, each bouquet of flowers, the wind chimes that sit above Daisy's plot and of course the wreath that will forever tell the world "Daisy ruler of the universe was here"

I'm not ashamed to say it, loosing Daisy nearly broke me, I never felt so alone

We've been weary poodle wranglers, inexperienced poodle wranglers and now shattered poodle wranglers

So, we did the only thing we could do, picked ourselves up, stood tall and tried to move forward....

CHAPTER 9

Now while I'm at this point, I would just add that many of us have lost poodles and we know the grief

We simply fall apart

However, I feel I must say that if a friend can see you at your lowest ebb - the low where you've been dragged through a tornado by your toes - and they still smile and hug you, then you know that friend is a keeper

The day after Daisy passed a knock came at my door

Yes, my hair was a splattered mess

Yes, I was in my pyjamas

Yes, my house looked like a bomb site

I opened the door and my friend Susan stood there with arms open

She'd drove down from near Morecambe

And in that one oh so small but massive gesture I felt such support

Yes, I looked an utter mess, but Susan didn't care

She came to "just be" and we drank tea and we chatted and all felt well

The moral to this is quite simply, good friends are so hard to find and if you've got one (or a few) then hang on to them

In fact, one of my good friends is in the US and many many times when my ideas for the poodle group run wild, she is the voice of reason

Treasure your friends xxx

CHAPTER 10

The summer was fast approaching and whilst we still mourned Daisy's loss, time would wait for no man or poodle

This year unlike last year we were booked and were definitely going to the caravan near Skegness

Excitement should have been building at poodle central

But instead, all we could feel was sadness,

Sadness Belle didn't make it to the beach one more time before she died

And sadness Daisy never made it to the beach one last time either

But....

We had Alfie, Teddy and Lupin and they were going to the beach

As usual in these affairs it's left to the packing fairies (me) to ensure all the clothes, leads, lotions and potions were packed ready for the car to be loaded

And as usual the day of loading was organised chaos....

Think Tetris I always say to Neil...slot it in like a jigsaw puzzle and as usual it falls on deaf ears

The car gets packed with everything thrown in!

Ok □

Everyone has a last pee pee

Last check -

Leads ☐

Water bowl ☐

Water ☐

Straighteners ☐

Right!

Everyone in!

Lupin at this stage is wondering if we are moving?

Remember she's never made the holiday trip before and is very quiet (which is soooooo not Lupin)

The gang are all in the car and secured

Ok!

Skegness here we come!

Now the trip normally takes about 3 hours with a poodle comfort stop in between

And I have to say we made excellent time and we were in the caravan before 4pm

Teddy and Alfie knew exactly where they were, even with Alfie's sight loss he knew the layout of the caravan

Lupin????

Well, the look she gave Me and Neil! anyone would think we'd dragged her to live in a tent!

However, after the initial nervousness she soon got into the caravan swing and totally amused herself running out one door on to the decking and running back in through the other door...

It was good to be back at the caravan

CHAPTER 11

Now whilst we are at the caravan we always try and meet up with poodle friends and have a walk together

It's a super event and always well attended, and the fact that Sandy often bakes delicious cakes for everyone to enjoy afterwards makes it just (pardon the pun) the icing on the cake!

Remember everyone had not seen each other for what felt such a long time so it was going to be a perfect day...

The day of the walk the British weather decided it was going to be unsettled ...however even the prediction of rain showers could not dampen us poodle walkers!

We all arrived at Theddlethorpe beach and the sun was shining!

Lupin saw a whole gang of poodles and immediately went all shy,

Off we set and as soon as we got onto the beach the heavens opened!

A gang of drenched poodle walkers we were

But even this could not stop the day

We walked, we chatted, and most importantly the poodles ran and had fun

Then with smiles on our faces we made our way back to Sandy's with the promise of yummy cakes

A truly lovely day was had by all and the time passed so quickly

That evening driving back to the caravan life felt good and we had 3 happy poodles with smiles on their faces

CHAPTER 12

When we are at the caravan, we mostly spend our time on various beaches letting the gang run free

However, this year thanks to Jenny we got to go and enjoy a "hidden" beach

It was soooo near the centre of Skegness but soooo hidden

And it was super quiet

We met Jenny and Tony and their standards Sasha and Poppy at the beach and Lupin came into her own!

She ran with the "big girls" and it was a wonderful sight to see

Alfie likes to meander these days so in order to keep walking forward Neil picked him up from time to time

Teddy just likes walking

It was a brilliant afternoon and one of the rare occasions we had a tired Lupin that evening

It's great when you get to go to these hidden gems and we are so lucky Jenny told us

The only regret is we didn't have more time to do more walks with them

A to do for next year's trip I think ☐

The nearly two weeks we spend in the caravan always passes so quickly and it feels like we've just got into our groove and we've got to pack up

So, after so much sun and fun we were on our way home again

Teddy went into his usual decline; he hates coming home from the caravan and is often found sulking for a day or two when we get home

As for Alfie and Lupin?

Well Alfie is a home bird really and enjoys coming back to a bigger bed lol

Lupin wasn't bothered a jot as it was a reunion of her stuffies who got left at home

The summer was finally treating us well

CHAPTER 13

We reached the end of July and ploughed into August with 3 happy poodles

The weather was holding and many days were spent enjoying the garden

Snakey had started to re-emerge and new characters were making their mark at poodle central

A drunken rooster called Randy had many of the tale followers in hysterics and mention the hedgehog mafia and there's not many who don't know the plot where they tried to frame poor Lupin!

Yes, all was looking good and a calm had settled over poodle central...

Now what have I said before ......that fate likes to play with us ...

CHAPTER 14

Well, we noticed Alfie was very restless,

He was up at night and drinking and pacing

I booked him in at the vets and as I wondered if his epiglottis flap was causing a problem - his tablets didn't seem to be "holding" his cough

I saw Vlad (yep that is his name) and Alfie was booked in for an X-ray and bloods the following week

However, we never even attended that appointment, things became a lot worse and quickly

After I saw Vlad, the morning after Alfie began being sick

Oh, he still had an appetite and ate his meals but as soon as he did, he was sick

If he drank water, he was sick

Something was off big time

We took Alfie back to the vets and it was decided to keep him in and find the root of the problem,

Ok I said he was due to come in for an X-ray in a couple of days anyways

Well, they scanned, they did blood tests, they x rayed him but they couldn't find out why Alfie couldn't eat anything without being sick

Alfie was admitted on the Sunday after I saw Vlad the previous Thursday, but by Tuesday the vets were still puzzled by Alfie's condition

He was losing weight

He was not settled

Now I did tell the vets that as Alfie can't see he relies on sound or voices - so it would be helpful if they just acknowledged him walking past his kennel - it did eventually get through to them and Alfie settled more

However, his condition was becoming dire

The vets told us they simply couldn't explain why Alfie's stomach wasn't emptying

It was acting normally but it was just building up hence Alfie being forced to keep being sick if he ate anything

Euthanasia was talked about - No way I said

Ok then we can try and pump his stomach and empty it and hope it settles

So, they anaesthetised Alfie and pumped his stomach empty

They fed Alfie and waited

We all waited - It wasn't good news ...

Alfie's stomach was not emptying and just filling up again

How long until it's full again I asked?

Maybe two days was the answer

Alfie had been in hospital nearly a week and we'd seen no improvement

We needed a miracle

CHAPTER 15

The vets telephoned on the Friday and the update wasn't good

Nothing had improved and they talked of pumping his stomach again

But to what end I said?

The other options were sending a camera down into Alfie's stomach, or the most drastic to open him up and try and find the problem with "eyes"

Initially we said OK to the camera, but when the earliest it could be done was the following week

We knew Alfie couldn't wait that long

So, the decision was made to open Alfie up and hope the problem would show itself

Now this was the riskiest option as Alfie was weak and he was 14

But the other option of doing nothing was simply something we couldn't do

These are the tough moments of poodle wrangling, you have to make the choices, and pray it's the right one

Now I know one of the vets thought our decision was wrong but I said to them what I always say

We will always give our Poogs the best possible fighting chance

So late Friday afternoon Alfie was taken down to surgery and we waited......

Alfie was in surgery about 2 1/2 hours in total

We received a call from the vets telling us they had found the problem and it could be repaired did we want to proceed?

Our resounding yes!

So, the problem was Alfie's tube at the bottom of his stomach had narrowed and the food simply couldn't get through to empty the stomach

The narrowing of the tube had not showed up on scans

A stent needed to be fitted

Alfie came through the surgery and because the vets were worried about him eating, a feeding tube was also placed at
the time of surgery

Oh, he looked like he'd done 20 rounds with a Doberman!

But he was still with us

CHAPTER 16

We picked Alfie up exactly one week after he'd been admitted and Yes, he had the vets creative grooming and Yes, he looked a little rough around the edges - But we were high fiving! - Alfie had battled through

The vet admitted our decision was the right one and that she thought it was very brave, Not brave I said, we had to do what was best for Alfie

But what we didn't understand was Alfie's new temporary feeding regime …. The feeding tube had been put into his neck and the food would go directly into his stomach

However, …. This involved us, puréed food and a whole heap of syringes

Alfie had to have the food syringed into his feeding tube at regular intervals and we had to flush the feeding tube prior to feeding and afterwards

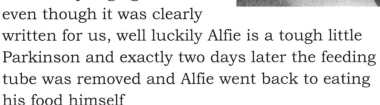

Neil was utterly convinced we were syringing too much even though it was clearly written for us, well luckily Alfie is a tough little Parkinson and exactly two days later the feeding tube was removed and Alfie went back to eating his food himself

Phew…We felt battered and bruised Poodle wranglers …but a trip was on the horizon ….

CHAPTER 17

Shortly before Alfie was poorly our friends Jacqueline and Olga offered us to use their caravan in South Wales

Neil had managed to get some time off so we thought let's go!

However, when Alfie became poorly, we wondered if a trip was really practical

But after the feeding tube was removed Alfie was doing really well eating and drinking, so once again we packed up the car fastened in the poodles and off we set

We'd never been to South Wales and thankfully Jacqueline had given us full instructions how to get to the caravan and if I am honest, we would never have found it so easily!

When we have been to Wales with the poodles we like to go and see some castles and this time was going to be no exception

We made a game of it

We spent all week trying to find a Welsh dragon, it was very tiring for Alfie but we took turns and carried him mostly

But when we went to the castle at Carmarthen even Alfie wandered about on his lead ...and Yes, we found the dragons lair!

It felt good to be silly and have fun after the recent trauma

We had a super week in Wales and as many of my friends will know not all my ideas are thought through...

When at one of the castle's, we visited the river by the side which had the original stepping stones used for hundreds of years enabling folk to cross from one side to the other ...

Ok I say to Teddy and Lupin

I pick them up one under each arm and started hopping and trotting over the stones...

It was only when I got two thirds over, I reached a stone I was worried about, its angle had me thinking the river was beckoning ....

I was saved though by a very nice Welshman who told me we're to put my foot and carried Teddy across

Yeah!!

We'd done it, we got across!!

We waved at Neil and Alfie

Only then did I realise we had to get back ......

Going back was much easier as I now knew how to handle the offending stone and I practically galloped across holding Teddy and Lupin

Tick that off our bucket list 🏴

The weather was glorious and I'm sure we'll be back next year chasing more dragons

CHAPTER 18

And once again my friends we are almost up to date and October is nearly gone

2021 has been full of ups and downs, tears and smiles, pain and joy

The festive season beckons and soon homes will be lit by shimmering fairy lights and hopes and dreams

I hope you've enjoyed sharing our year and whatever 2022 has in store for us all

I'm sure we will face it head on and in Lupin's case run straight at it x

Part 4
Who's Randy Rooster?

CHAPTER 1

♥Good Morning from Poodle Central♥

Its bed changing day here today and poor Miss Daisy has been photo-snapped!

Bad mum has snapped her photo with a bed head

Teddy and Alfie quickly fled the scene as Daisy doesn't authorise these "un coiffured photos" 👻

Please be safe in the knowledge that Daisy's ears are now brushed and back to Daisy standard

CHAPTER 2

♥Good Morning from Poodle Central♥

There's a cloud of dust here at the moment as I'm calmly sat having my cup of tea ....

Why you ask??

Well, I made the unfortunate mistake of saying let's tidy those scruffy faces....

The signal for mass poodle galloping!
Seriously .... anyone would think I was thinking about mass scalping ...

So now I sit, cup of tea
Clippers on charge

Being glared at by Daisy and Teddy

Where's Alfie you ask? Well, he's sat next to me cause poor Alf can't see the clippers 😕

Never mind Alf, you'll look all handsome with your shaved face later 🖤

CHAPTER 3

♥<u>Good morning From Poodle Central</u>♥

And it's all about the belly rubs this morning ...

Now Daisy was offered a belly rub but she Erm refused on the grounds –

It's not cool that 'ruler of the universe' is on their back with their legs up in the air...

Alfie enjoyed his belly rub with a big smile, but I have to say the belly rub star of the moment was the Tedster

Now Teddy got right into that rub and his little legs were a kicking in delight ....

The moral?
Teddy says his dad might be a demon number picker but he's got magical belly rubbing hands 😊

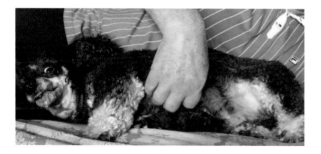

CHAPTER 4

♥*Good Evening from Poodle Central*♥

Steak 🐾 for the
gang's dinner

As you can see
Daisy came
running

CHAPTER 5

♥Good Evening from Poodle Central♥

This is what being in the dog house looks like...
Yes ...

The Tedster, is giving me the cold shoulder...

Why? You cry?

Well, I cleaned his potato 🥔ear today with wipes and lotion
Got the wax out

And did the Tedster appreciate my work?
Nope

He walked in the living room and turned his backside to me...
Sigh...

Loving a poodle 🖤is never easy

Quick update...

Teddy lasted all of 5 mins and came for some loving

Love You Tedd's

CHAPTER 6

♥*Good Afternoon from Poodle Central*♥

Simone 1
Poodle Gang minus 1

The Alfie has been captured and finally had his
face and feet and tail done ✔

La! La!
I'm making my stealthy move on the Tedster ....

Daisy will be last
Wish me luck 👍👍👍👍

CHAPTER 7

♥*Good Afternoon from Poodle Central*♥

Well as you can see the little Parkinson's were less than co-operative to have their photos taken....

Heck I was lucky I managed to corral them into getting their scraggy faces shaved!

Raspberries all round from the Tedster
Diva strop from Daisy
And indignant from Alfie

At present they are now all acting like dying swans and glaring at me .... their dad giving them sympathy...

Funny how I'm always the bad cop 😄😄😄

CHAPTER 8

♥*Good Morning from Poodle Central*♥

So, the hour going back has caused pandemonium here....🐾🐾🐾
Daisy's internal clock went off at her 6am which was of course now 5am ....and no amount of me telling her of this change convinced her I was right and she was wrong...So up we get

And then we had the medication debate ...remember this is 5am
Her Keppra was due at 6am and her 8 hours had passed, but the clock going back was telling me a different story

In the end Daisy rolled her eyes and subtlety encouraged me to bring the moral debate to a close as she wanted to return to her duvet

Ok one shot of Keppra
And Daisy's away, back to bed
The zzzzzz

Half hour later I feel Alfie sat up
Quickly reciting the "go back to sleep" prayer
Nope
He's moving around
"Alf go back to sleep it's not 6 yet"
No, he's off the bed
Ok he wants a drink
Yes!!!! I can hear him having a drink, he will get back on the bed soon
I settle back

Daisy's snoring
Teddy's buried under the quilt with camel 🐪(
don't ask 😃)
And then that noise every poodle lover dreads....
The poodle feet going downstairs when everyone
else is in bed!

Yep, the Alf is up ...
Ok Neil let's Alfie out for a wee
Back upstairs
Right Bo! Bo's!
Er No....
Alfie's up and looking for a target ...er I mean
someone to take him on

He's flat on his back legs a going rolling around
Me silently thinking God I wish this bed was wider
Pulls Daisy towards me – gets a grumbling

Alf's in full leg throw ....
And bam! Lands a high right kick into the mound
that is Teddy!
The mound jumps!
The quilt is pulled!

I'm holding onto the quilt and Daisy as the Teddy
is rapidly exiting his comfy spot
Alfie sits down, his work is done

Teddy jumps back on the bed scowling at Alfie
It's now just after 6.30
Right!!! That's it!
Let's just have another hour!

All settled
So now it's just after 9am and the little
Parkinson's are singing the *zzzzz*

Dam that clock change...😃

CHAPTER 9

♥Good Morning from Poodle Central♥

Or should I scream towers

The post decided after months of delivering when they felt like it or delivering at 6pm they would start knocking at 7.30!

Well que a poodle annoyed bark.... they are not keen on having their beauty sleep interrupted However, one poodle didn't get the memo and decided alert bark actually meant running around on full scream

I can assure you it's not cool when said poodle jumps onto the bed screaming like a siren!

And the poodle?
Yes, Miss Lupin

Even Daisy awoke at this Hoo Har,
Alfie and Teddy shut up and watched her
It was a one-woman air raid sound ...
Lupin ssshh

She's stood on her legs looking out the window to check that the offending red van has pulled away

Me awake
Lupin

She looks at me, at Alfie, at Teddy (Daisy had thought by this stage Lupins off her rocker and gone back to sleep) and calmly trots off the bed and goes in search of her dad

Yes, I'd say she's found her voice 😐
The moral of the story?
Ear plugs are such a good idea when you've a
sister called Lupin 😄😄

CHAPTER 10

♥Breaking news from Poodle Central!!!♥

We've snakey action! 🐍

It's bitter sweet and I'm shedding a tear here for my Boo 😿

But snakey has been dragged out of hibernation by Lupin

She walked up to snakey and grabbed him then gave the resting snakey a big ol shake

Teddy was on high alert!

Rest assured no Snakeys were harmed during this full-on assault

However, Teddy has now escorted snakey back to his hole

CHAPTER 11

Now everyone knows Teddy is the family's thinker...

He's watched Lupin

He's watched Lupin giving snakey  a scragging

He's thought about it

Well last night he laid on rug near Lupin
And tonight, he's laid next to Lupin

I'd say the Teddy is thinking Lupin is ok

CHAPTER 12

♥Good Morning from a wet Poodle Central♥

As everyone knows poodles are famously water dogs, well someone forgot to send the memo to my lot 😐

They turn into doomsday commandos in wet weather, planning each pee pee trip with military precision in order to feel the least damp 💧💧💧

Que the 6 o'clock roll call!
Alfie and Teddy showed their faces and Alfie sniffed up smelling that rain at the living room doorway

He was about to turn about when Neil said "ah ah ah!"

Both boys begrudgingly went and full filled their duty with only a slight scowl at us

Now the girls...
Well Daisy is well known as a rain dancer and successfully avoids the rain (unless of course it's lashing it down, then she looks like a soggy piece of cotton wool 🐩)

Lupin we have found will only go when she absolutely needs to and is not into pee shopping So out they go ...

Daisy doing her bit for the cause and Lupin, well watching she'd decided she might go around 8 Cup of tea and back up stairs

To be met by snoring!
Oh yes, the little Parkinson's had settled right
back down grabbing the best spots in the bed and
a force 10 Gale wasn't for moving them

So as any good poodle wrangler would, cup of tea
in hand I took my spot perched on the end and
rolled my eyes yet again, how it's ended up I'm
under the paw 🐾

The moral?...

A wise poodle wrangler would start running back
upstairs whilst said little Parkinson's are pee
peeing 😜😜

And for anyone wondering how Daisy had beat me
upstairs? and got back on the bed?

Oh simple...she got her dad to take her straight
back upstairs (he's well trained!)

CHAPTER 13

♥*Good Evening from Poodle Central*♥

Well Lupin decided today was the day she needed to bond with Daisy....

Daisy was a twirling on the rug, hoping to catch the eye for someone to play and enter stage right was Lupin ...

Now Lupin is twice the size of Daisy
So off she sets 100 mile an hour to play with Daisy,
Daisy see this Lupin -a-motion coming at her and sidesteps

Que much running and side stepping
Daisy finally getting tired of the game and telling Lupin what for

Lupin just accepts and moves onto lamb chop, Daisy goes for 40 winks

Teddy strolling in

CHAPTER 14

♥*Good Morning from Poodle Central*♥

Well, if we wanted a quiet life, I'm guessing we should have decided we were going to live with goldfish instead of poodles 😀

Apparently 6am is the new 9am in Lupin's book and with a willing accomplice called Alfie, she's on a roll!

Up and down the stairs like a good un, bouncing on the bed
Teddy got up off the bed, threw the noisy duo a scowl (totally wasted on Alfie mind) and marched into his hole, dragging back what appeared to be a snakey tail

Now as kipping is taken very seriously by Daisy, Lupin and Alfie were both very careful to try and avoid the sleeping white ball

However, God love her Lupin we've seen runs and forgets what her legs are doing - so que a few near misses of the Lupini's legs!

Eventually everyone settled and a sigh was heard (from me 😌)

But come 8am when the workmen arrived the boys closely followed by Lupin all ran to give a warning bark (howl in Lupin's case) to ensure Poodle Central wasn't about to be tarmacked

Such is the joy...

I turned to Daisy who was still flat out
Are you getting up?
Daisy lifts her head

We hear the sound of legs on the stairs...
I look at Daisy
And then 3 damp poodles jump on the bed and
make their presence felt

Daisy lifts her head
Growls

All 3 poodles look and skulk off to sit down
Daisy satisfied her work is done, gets up looks at
me - and we're up 😄

The moral?

Size doesn't matter, it's what you say that does

CHAPTER 15

♥Good Morning from Poodle Central♥

And I'm here to report that Miss Lupin has found a new game...
And I'm it 🙈

Oh yeah, 6am time for Daisy's Keppra and both Alfie and Lupin are wide awake and ready to go ...
It's not up time I say to them ...

Both look at me if I'm slightly addled 😕
No, c'mon Bo Bo time
Well Lupin had found her own way of getting me up now ....

And what you cry? licking? bouncing? playing?
No to all the above

The daft muppet gets on my pillow and pulls on my hair ... oh not big clumps I add, just strands 🙈...
Oh yes, she finds this whole thing highly amusing
I can say I'm not there with her on this amusement 😐

So, if I ignore her, she twangs a few more strands
Pack it in Lupin, at this rate when I go to the hairdressers they'll be asking about my "thin spot"

Lupin just looks at me - strand of my much-loved hair dangling from her mouth

Anyway, this morning I fooled her!

Daisy Keppra
Back in bed ✅
Tells Alfie and Lupin it's not up time ✅
Daisy and Teddy happily singing the *zzzz* ✅
Que Lupin
And Ta Da!
No, she couldn't get my hair!
Cause I'd pulled a bob hat on!

Simone - 1
Lupin- 0
😂😂😂

Ask Lupin it's just not the same trying to pull a bob hat
The only downside was Daisy looking at me like "who the hell are you?!??"

And the moral?

In order to be a professional poodle wrangler you need to stay one step ahead of the scamps 😂😂😂

CHAPTER 16

♥*Good Evening from Poodle Central*♥

We start a busy week tomorrow ...

26th Thursday Daisy celebrates
her 17th birthday
28th Saturday Lupin celebrates
her 1st Birthday
30th Monday Alfie celebrates his
14th Birthday

Cakes ordered ✅
Balloons ordered (let's hope they
arrive) ✅
Let the merrymaking begin

CHAPTER 17

♥*Good Afternoon from Poodle Central*♥

I know many of you had hoped for a new
snakeynapper with the arrival of Lupin,
And yes, she has dragged snakey 🐌 in a total
undignified snakey fashion 🙁

But Lupin will find her own paws 🐾
Snakey I'm sure will still feature in the tales 🐌
And it seems at the minute trying to thwart me
and my hair is high on her agenda ...along with a
one poodle mission to destuff anything that
doesn't move 🙄🙄

There was and can only ever be One
Snakeynapper ....and her memory will remain
bright 🐕🐌🖤

In the meantime, I can
advise you Samantha that
the poodle shower cap
offered no protection from
the Loony
Hairdresser...she flipped it
off and settled down to
chew (much like we see
some chewing tobacco) on a clump of my hair 🐩

Luckily all she wanted was a chew and all my hair
is still intact

Daisy on the other hand is seriously not
impressed with my headwear ...it's given her a
start twice up to now 🐩🐩🐩

CHAPTER 18

♥*Good afternoon from Poodle Central*♥

Daisy's swim day ....
Minding her own business, swimming up and
down

Then splash!!!!
Lupin jumped in the bath too, not to be left out...

Daisy?... is nothing sacred?!?!?

CHAPTER 19

♥First of Daisy's birthday photos! ♥

Opening the cards and presents and greeting her balloons
Many thanks to all who sent her a card
Kentucky chicken later and Cakey

Big thanks to – Ruth, Paul and Teddy
Susan, Jason and Bronski
Lesley,
Sarah, Charlie and Lottie
Janette, Peter and Holly
Rach
Auntie Sue for eating cakey 😉

CHAPTER 20

Good Afternoon from Poodle Central...

Today we celebrate Daisy's 17th Birthday!
This little bundle of white fluff has brought me
endless days of joy...

Now you'd think that today we would be
celebrating and enjoying Daisy's Day...

However, the Lupini didn't get the memo 😕
I went upstairs and threw a couple of unicorns
downstairs to throw in the washer ...

Me shouting I'll not be long... and looked ...mouth
hanging open...
There at the bottom of the stairs was one Lupin
enjoying herself as the "stuffy monster" de stuffing
a unicorn!

And the little scamp even tried de stuffing it again
as I put the stuffing back in to clear it up

The moral?

Never, ever leave
a quiet Lupin
alone 😃😃😃😃

CHAPTER 21

♥*Good Morning from Poodle Central*♥

And it's the day after the party ● before

And as you can see Miss Daisy is chilling today ....
after stuffing herself on Kentucky Chicken 🍗

Alfie, Teddy and Lupin are also relaxing ...but
being a wise poodle wrangler, I have one eye on
the Stuffy monster 😊

CHAPTER 22

♥*Happy 1st Birthday to Lupin!* ♥

Miss Lupin only arrived with us earlier this month, but she's wiggled herself into her spot with her sister and brothers....

And let us know she's a stuffy monster
This fun-loving hairdresser who took Teddy's snakey out for a walk 😵‍💫🧻

Happy Birthday our beautiful Lupini! 🍫🍫🍫🍫

She'll be having her balloons and cakey later, with her choice of dinner...Daisy whispering Kentucky Chicken 🍗😄🐾🐾🐾🐾

CHAPTER 23

♥Good Evening from Poodle Central♥

Sunday is now designated as a day of rest ...

Miss Lupin has thoroughly enjoyed her Birthday and all the little Parkinson's are now currently "flat out" after stuffing themselves

I've advised them that tomorrow a "Skelton service" will be available as this morning running around getting ready to go pick up Lupins balloons  and cake I mis-stepped on the top of the stairs and fell flat on my kisser!...

Yes, my ego and my shins were bruised but nothing would have stopped me getting Lupins big day done
Daisy rolled her eyes at me...

The moral?

for the love of God let me remember to pick my feet up when running 🏃

CHAPTER 24

♥*Good Morning from Poodle Central*♥

Now I did send a memo out to the poodle horde that Sunday was now a rest day, however the poodle committee apparently read it and blew "raspberries!"

So early this morning we had a very excited Lupin charging back up the stairs after having a pee pee She was all wet

Why you ask?

Well, the Lupini gets super excited when she does a pee pee and plows back into the house at break neck speed, sadly for her this speed has no brakes …

So, in she comes behind Teddy,
No brakes
Plows right through the water bowl, water 💧up high - splashing down on a still running Lupin and catching a very "put out" Teddy

Que 2 poodles now running back to the bed and jumping on
Shaking …

Waking up a very miffed Daisy who immediately airs her displeasure at the damp twosome

Lupin and her top knot looking very bedraggled
Were they finished?
No 🙄🙄

Lupin then decides to grab Teddy's camel 🐫, get it singing and proceeds to run around with the camel singing

Teddy's off the bed doing exactly what Lupin wants, heck she's not even fussed about camel 🐫anymore she just likes being chased 😃

Me - you 2 pack it in!
Lupin skulks off to find her dad

Teddy drags camel back into his hole with snakey and makes (for dramatic effect) the biggest sigh...

And where you ask was Alfie when these wacky races were taking place?

Alfie was taking his time coming back upstairs and timed it perfectly to miss the water and the camelathon

He jumps back on the bed and settles down and starts with the zzzzzz

Me .... thinking let's all just settle

Daisy gets up, gives me a swipe, apparently, it's up time now 😃😃

The moral?

Only the brave become Poodle Wranglers....only the brave 🐩🐩🐩🐩

CHAPTER 25

♥Good Afternoon from Poodle Central♥

It's high drama here today!
Well, it's Alfie's birthday and he gets to choose his choice of dinner....

Now it's come quite a shock to Daisy ruler of the universe that Alfie's first choice isn't ...gulp Kentucky Chicken 🎈

Apparently, Daisy dismissed the memo saying the Birthday boy/girl gets to choose

Well, the Alf's first choice will always be a MacDonald's 🍟

A double cheeseburger 🍔hold the sauces and pickle and a taste of MacFluffy ice cream for afters...

So, we're bracing ourselves for a sulky Daisy later 😕

Lupin and Teddy aren't fussed one jot! they say this Birthday Train 🚂can just keep on going.... they are loving the treats

Big thanks to everyone for his cards and core biscuits
And Sarah for his Stuffie

And Alfie says Thank you for his birthday wishes
😊😊😊

CHAPTER 26

♥Good Evening from Poodle Central♥

It's official the Lupin is a Poogmole....she came a galloping up this evening with the gang and immediately wanted to go under the quilt ...

2 seconds later one Lupin snuggled under the quilt kicking her legs out to make her space,

Now my legs are up slightly to allow air, I'm bent to allow Alfie and Daisy curled in my arm

Phew .... Teddy always starts Bo Bo time in his hole or I would be wound like a "new age" art sculpture

So, it's night night from Us

CHAPTER 27

♥*Good Evening from Poodle Central*♥

It's been Christmas excitement here today as the little Parkinson's help decorate the tree...

Each one hanging their own decoration on the tree, decorating the tree is an important tradition here and no one is ever forgotten

Frank, Jack, Christie, Jakey and now our Belley Boo 😢
This year however Teddy did the honours of

hanging Belle's decoration 🖤
Lupin hung her first decoration 🌲
Neil hung "the believe Bell 🔔"
So here we have it, the tree of 2020 🌲

CHAPTER 28

Merry Christmas from Poodle Central....

All the stockings are hung and Lupin now has her own stocking in time for Santa courtesy of Auntie Beth and Auntie Stevie

CHAPTER 29

Good Evening from Poodle Central....

Daisy here,

Well, Lupini is feeling more herself,
Me? I said "high five!"

I've told Santa it might be a goer!

Here the gang are having lamb on Christmas Day
- our Dad bought us a leg from Asda 😊😊

No Turkey for this Daisy!

Anyway, my mum picked up our new car today so
we're all set!

Skegness here we come July 2021!

I say Merry Christmas Everyone!
Oh, and PS, best not come a calling at Poodle
Central, my mum and dad have had garlic!

CHAPTER 30

We're a little late this year with our Christmas photos

It's been hard to take them

Well anyway here at Poodle Central Santa did come and the gang opened their presents 🎁

Teddy is now the proud owner of a raft of hedgehogs 🦔(who kept arriving all day 😊)

Lupini has her very own snakey 🐍

Alfie has a new gnome ...even though Santa brought the wrong size, (Lupin has been eyeing it up)

And Daisy now has her Kentucky gift card

CHAPTER 31

Good Evening from Poodle Central....

Daisy here, I'm liking this updating and think I'm rather good at it

Well Santa called at Poodle Central and now we have an army of hedgehogs everywhere, of course the Tedster is beyond himself and thinks life is good
Me, I think

Alfie got a new gnome, but this gnome is XXL and is as tall as Alf!

Lupini thought the whole shebang was super fun and is now the proud owner of her very own purple snakey
Now what she chooses to do with snakey will be anyone's guess, but I can tell you she was certainly charmed by Teddy's hedgehogs!

My mum has done her best she misses the Boo and cried this morning cause the Boo wasn't here
I keep telling her Belle is always with us, it's just we can't hold her

And now All is quiet....
Teddy and Lupin have pigged out on Vanilla
And we noshed through our joint of lamb
So Merry Christmas All
From Me and All at Poodle Central

Love Daisy

CHAPTER 32

Good Morning from Poodle Central....

Well apparently, one of the poodles' hordes didn't read the Boxing Day memo 😄

The one that said "let's have a nice lie in and no chewing your mum's hair"

So, our hyper charged Lupini decided she didn't need to go to sleep but would search out all the new stuffies and rate them in order of noise 😶

She did try to get the Tedster involved in this important work, but a wander into his hole ●only resulted in Teddy grumpily telling her to come back when it's day light …

Alfie and Daisy were flat out and Lupin had no chance in waking them

Besides Daisy's still holding a small grudge to her now hormone balanced sister 😄

So, it was left to Lupin to take on for the team - mental note no sugar for Lupin late at night 😄

So, this morning as we went downstairs for early morning pee pee's Lupini's work was apparent ….

All Teddy's hedgehogs 🦔had been thrown to the back of the sofa - a bit like hedgehog netball 😶
And fair play to Lupin she'd scored a slam dunk as all were now in some fashion balanced on the sofa back
Teddy???

Well, he went to do his business then calmly jumped on the sofa and stood on his back legs pulling said hedgehogs back to his cushion

Once done, jumped down and ran back to bed
Daisy watched this and promptly went over to her nest to check on her "itty bitty" which had survived the Lupini whirlwind

All was quiet
And even Lupin settled down for a nice 40 winks

It was only later Alfie could be heard moaning ...
C'mon Alf settle down
No, still moaning

Alf!...
wait hang on he's not on the bed

Sigh... up we get, in search of the Alf who was in the back room
Staring up at a rather messy bed (thanks Lupin) and in the middle of the bed was ...yep Alfie's new gnome 😫

Gets gnome, gives to Alfie who drags it back to bedroom
Sure I think, what's one more on the bed 🙄🙄
On he gets ... me plopping gnome next to him
Ok .... And let's all have 40 winks

Ring! Ring! Ring!
Me 😱😱😱

My sister calling and then hanging up by the time I got there
Right ...we're up! 😄😄😄😄

CHAPTER 33

Neil took Teddy and Lupin to the park this
morning
Enjoyed a lovely trot round,
Teddy did some sniffing
Lupin did some mooching

So, as they get back to the
car park a car pulled up and
out got an older couple
They open boot and out
bounds a spaniel

Neil walking towards car park entrance
And the old bloke then decides to use one of those
ball chucker's and throws it towards Neil, Teddy
and Lupin - So now we have an off-lead spaniel
hurtling 100 miles an hour towards them

Teddy discreetly places himself behind Neil
Poor Lupin didn't as she was busy sniffing, Said
spaniel throws itself towards Lupin
Lupin jumps a mile and starts barking
And the old bloke????

Starts to tell Neil to get that barking dog under
control!! 💀💀

Me?... I'd have thrown that
bloody ball right at him!
Neil tells the old bloke, to read
the signs

All dogs must be on a lead and
what kind of d*** throws a ball
near a car park! so shut your
mouth!

Lupin....I love my dad

CHAPTER 34

Good Morning from Poodle Central....

Well apparently, it's New Year's Day today 🐱

And here at Poodle Central it's a bigger event
It's Teddy's birthday!

Yep, our little man is 9!

The thinker of the family will today enjoy his
homemade special trifle (no fruit or sponge) made
my his auntie Sue

Daisy is already telling Teddy the benefits of a
Kentucky Chicken 🍗a day 😀🐔

Now it will be touch and go whether Teddy's
balloons 🎈 are here, but 👍 👍 👍

I remember bringing our Tedster home, we
travelled a way for him and just off a photo and a
gut feeling

He's the sweetest hedgehog 🦔loving little man and
now thanks to Lupin has 2 snakes 🐍in his hole
(now that's another story
for another day)

Happy Birthday Teddy

We love you 😇

CHAPTER 35

Good Evening from Birthday Poodle Central...

Well sadly Teddy's balloon 🎈 didn't arrived 😟
But his trifle has 🖤

And I thought I'd share this morning's snakey
🐾action

Lupin is no stealth snakeynapper ...buts that's ok
as there was only one snakeynapper 🐾🖤

Lupins a full frontal let's go for it wrestler ... in
fact I think I recognise one of her moves from a
famous wrestler 🎵🤕

She's taken pink snakey upstairs
And here this morning it was full on snakey
wrestling
Note Teddy's face

Then off to the park - sadly no squirrels 🐿were
about

And lastly here's Teddy's trifle

There will be no
talking to the little
man later

CHAPTER 36

Neil and the girls

Daisy and her big little sister Lupin
Matching pink hoodies 🐾🐾
(And look everyone! Neil does have a smile 😄)

CHAPTER 37

Good Morning from Poodle Central....

It's been a little quiet here (I'm not complaining lol)

The little Parkinson's have been snuggling on down
However, I thought I'd share this to give a smile today.

As many know poor Lupin had a phantom pregnancy in December and turned into Raging Lupini 🙀

Well, the galastop erm put a stop to that and all settled ...but since we've had a little morning ritual here at Poodle Central ...

Erm "titty watch" 😕😕

Which basically was checking on Lupin's teats ensuring they were receding
And they are 😊

Our little Lupin's hormones are back to normal
Now Lupin says enough is enough...she's convinced Teddy just wants a quick thrill look 😕

Ahhh poodle wrangling ...it will be fun they said ...
It's never dull with 4 🐩🐩🐩🐩

CHAPTER 38

All knackered

CHAPTER 39

Good Afternoon from Poodle Central....

Daisy is not well 🙁
She who must be obeyed had an off tummy yesterday and had some milk of magnesia...

Her grumbly tummy settled, but she had a very restless night and needed a little extra Keppra

Alfie is snuggled on the sofa with her and she's eaten her breakfast and had a poo...

But my little princess is very tired 💤
Teddy and Lupin have tried to be quiet...but it's incredibly hard when you're an action-packed Lupini

They've been to the park and enjoyed skidding on the ice with their dad 🙂

I think a day of loving is in order and a watchful eye

CHAPTER 40

Good Afternoon from Poodle Central....

As you can see, we've had Stuffie Armageddon here this morning here...

And the culprits?
Well, The Lupini and Tedzini

Now Teddy is daft as brush with Lupin and allows the wrestler to launch her moves on him ....

Only when he's had enough, he makes a dash for the sofa (or his Dad if he's home)

I can officially say that chicken now is destuffed and if Lupin had her way, he'll also have his danglers pulled out too!

Add this to the arrival of the postman and thankfully now all are having 40 winks (and recharging 🔋)

Ahh now when was life quiet???

CHAPTER 41

Good Evening from Poodle Central....

Daisy is doing good,
She's got another vet appointment next
Wednesday with Hanna

She's my total superstar
and has been swimming
today and had a bark with
the gang

She currently sporting a
"Daisy Corn" to keep the
hair out of her face

Currently all little
Parkinson's are sending the zzzzzz

Tomorrow we will hear the tale of how Teddy has
2 snakeys in his hole

CHAPTER 42

Good Morning from Poodle Central....

Well, I've been asked about the tale of 2 snakeys a few times now ....so here goes
At Christmas Lupin received her very own purple snakey from Santa

Exactly the same as snakey but purple - so we think she's a girl 😊

Lupin thoroughly enjoyed Miss snakey and

dragged her
around the
kitchen and
living room
However, Teddy
wouldn't engage
with her ☹️

Well, the day after Boxing Day arrived and as normal it was a free for all on the bed with toys

Me having my cup of tea ☕
Now Lupin is no stealth Lupin, if she goes to Teddy's hole, she makes a bold assault and tries to march in

Whether she succeeds is another matter 😊
Well Daisy was a kipping
Alfie was settled with his gnome and Teddy was laid on the bed with Lupin messing around with a crocodile 🐊(don't ask)

Anyways she jumped off the bed and Teddy went into high alert 🔔thinking a hole attack was coming....

However, the Lupin trotted past Teddy's hole and carried on downstairs
Teddy looking ...

Shortly thereafter Lupin arrives back upstairs with Miss Snakey 🐍
Teddy still glaring from inside his hole

Well Lupin promptly drags Miss Snakey up to Teddy's hole and pushes her towards the Tedster...
Teddy 😊😊😊.... well, he grabs Miss snakey and pulls her in his hole

Lupin, happy at this development jumps back in the bed and starts sidling
up to Alfie and his gnome...
Teddy ...can be heard
rustling around in his hole
So, we now have 2 Snakeys
🐍🐍and a camel in Teddy's
hole and the game is on...

It's not covert...It's not stealth...

It's Lupin style and that's how it should be, and Lupin decided that all Snakeys should be together

Until that is when she makes a run at the morning and drags (well tries) snakey and Miss snakey out

She has Teddy running this way and then dragging wayward Snakeys 🐍🐍back into his hole, and that my friends is exactly how the Tedster likes it 🐍🖤

CHAPTER 43

Thank God the ice has gone on the patio......

Lupin is no Torvill and Dean

Her legs go everywhere

I've never seen someone who's legs are going 100 mile an hour and not getting anywhere

No, we are not entering the next Olympics

CHAPTER 44

Good Morning from Poodle Central....

Well apparently, Lupins built in alarm clock doesn't have a snooze for her mums poorly tooth setting...

All was quiet and life was good, until I felt this rustling above my head ...I was just about to question 'hang on who is on my head' when Lupin threw her head back and went into full wolf howl!

Even Daisy looked up at the over excited Lupini

When my hearing came back ...I opened my eyes to the sight of Lupins belly - she was stood akimbo across my head

There's nobody there!

Lupin turned and looked at me and suddenly I felt very conscious I should had brushed my hair before going to bed

The look she was giving me was definitely rating my rather bedraggled appearance

Me marches up to the blinds....

Now a full poodle audience

Lupin silently saying I wouldn't do that if I were you ...

And ta! da! opens the blinds to be greeted by the window cleaner going about his business quite happily until he sees me wild woman of Borneo and her poodle army ...

Lupin, Teddy and Alfie fly at the window
All howls and tongues a slobbering ...

Me? given up trying to look cool 😎
Wishing I could slide under Daisy and disappear...

Ah well, grabs my fleece

Strolls downstairs, secures the raging poodles
(Daisy asked me to point out she was not one of
them) and pay the window cleaner

Ooh you caught me unawares I say

Window cleaner...doesn't know where to look
It's a nice day says I

Behind me the living room door is rattling - the
poodles want out

Window cleaner...well, see you next time
Me shutting gates

And opens door

And they're out!

Running looking for the interloper who had the
cheek to look through our windows
Cup of tea

Mental note...do not open the blinds when your
hair looks like Kate bush 😳

CHAPTER 45

Daisy has had her vet check
Hanna is a lovely vet, she's always so caring with
my lot

Re Daisy's Keppra she can have an additional
extra dose if and when required

We decided not to up her dose from 0.1ml
Now....Daisy's teeth have a lot of plaque on them
(hang my head in shame) but they are causing no
discomfort or pain, so no action there either

Daisy says she wants something good for her tea
now!

CHAPTER 46

Good Morning from Poodle Central.....

See as a professional poodle wrangler, you'd think I'd be able to say by now "seen it all"

Well maybe If I was wrangling terriers!
Poodle wrangling is not for the faint hearted; these fur balls keep you on your toes!

This morning all was well...
Neil trotted off to work
The poodles barely lifted their head to wave "ta! ta!"
Everyone quite happily dozing

Now my poogy sense didn't start tingling (mental note best check that out)
Although Lupin did take herself off downstairs, I made the rookie poodle wrangling mistake that "she's ok, she's quiet"

So, as we all tramp downstairs for a morning cup of tea ☕ and a morning pee pee break, I really shouldn't have been surprised at what greeted me in the hall

A scattering of green stuffing....
Me 😨😨

Enters living room and there you go!
My draft excluder had been attacked!

Now Lupins looking very casual here, and doesn't acknowledge the now partially destuffed draft excluder...

Instead, she trots towards the toy box and proceeds to dig, perhaps looking for the hope diamond maybe?? 😬
Me? gets my cup of tea

And wonders how on earth I was taken by such a rookie thought?

There's no such thing as a quiet poodle that's not up to mischief 😄

And as I'm sat writing this, I see Lupin now stood in the toy box 📦intent on dragging every single stuffy out,
taking inventory maybe?

To see which she's not had a go at ragging ...

Now the question is...does gin taste alright when poured into tea? 😄😄

<u>CHAPTER 47</u>

Good Evening from Poodle Central...

I broke the news today to Lupin she's having her
Spay on Wednesday....

She told me back
"Can I call you a bad mum"

I said "sweetie you can call me what you want,
your still being spayed"

Now maybe that explains Lupin galloping upstairs
after her tea and ragging Neil's shoes and
throwing Miss snakey around.

Sigh....toddlers....

CHAPTER 48

2 boys and a gnome

CHAPTER 49

Good Evening from Poodle Central....

Lupin has been fitted into her dinosaur Babygro today

A little adjusting and ta! da!

Normal service is resuming.... she thoroughly enjoyed ripping up an envelope, watched by Daisy who just rolled her eyes

Now there's a little queue forming while their dad dishes up dinner.... hearts

CHAPTER 50

Just hanging with my big sis
Daisy & Lupin

CHAPTER 51

Good Afternoon from Poodle Central......

It's been a little quiet here at HQ
The gang have been commissioning a petition for
me to bring back the sun ☀(I have tried
explaining to them I can't control the weather but
have you ever tried arguing with a mob of
determined poodles?) 😄

Anyways the weather
debate aside, Lupin is
back running on all
cylinders and
apparently the vet has is completely wrong -
trying to throw yourself off the sofa, is in fact
highly recommended as a healing method 🙌

Queue many footballing "saves" trying to prevent
Lupin launching.... Yesterday the mischievous
Lupin decided she wanted to "nibble" my nose 😐
So today I'm sporting a rather red nose 👃

On the upside all the little
Parkinson's are Knick knack
knackered and all is quiet at
poodle central.... until 3am
when the Lupini's batteries
recharge 🔋
Daisy says that's it!
Lupin better not try interrupting her poogy sleep
tonight 😾, Teddy and Alfie say "Rah! Daisy!"
So, a cup of tea ☕
And the moral?
Remember quiet is never possible when you live
with poodles .... neither are lie ins!

CHAPTER 52

Good Afternoon from Poodle Central....

Well, I sent a memo to the poodle horde that a quiet day was in order today ....

To let Daisy catch up and rest up ...

However as usual the Lupini failed to read the memo, instead going old school and eating it...

So as Daisy was a napping z^z and Teddy and Alfie were chilling the Lupin was on a mischief mission...

She's already chewed one of the wicker toy box handles so I ended up cutting it off and hoped it would amuse her for (rolls eyes) a little while ...
Nope!
Ok off she slinked

Hang on I'm not being caught again, a quiet Lupini is never good (unless I can see her) so I go looking for her,

And yep.... sat amid my sketchers.... now missing their insole
Sighs...

Ok they were old ones; you can have them Lupin Queue a few hours of a happy Lupin throwing and chewing my shoes

After the rug was full of insole, I decided a Hoover was in order...
I hoovered rug and was given the stink eye

Now I always unplug the Hoover when I'm not using it

Well, it's a good job I did otherwise the Lupin might have been sporting a different mop-a-top 🫣

Yes, the little ###% had a chew on my Hoover cable!
A few choice words!

Lupin looking at me "what???"
Never tell me it's a quiet life with poodles 😵😵

On the upside Daisy has had a lovely lazy day, keep on feeling well my little girl

And finally, Lupin is having 5 minutes too

CHAPTER 53

Lupini V the Gnome

Lupini - 1
Gnome - 0

Emergency...surgery for
Gnome!

CHAPTER 54

Daisy likes me singing to her when she has her meals...

Me? - whatever she wants

Well, this morning she's enjoyed her breakfast while I sang the drifters

Now... she's enjoying 40 winks

CHAPTER 55

Today has brought me much joy....

Right back when we first brought Jack home to be a friend for Frank, all I ever wanted was my fur balls to bond

And along the way each and every one has and I've been an incredibly proud Poodle Wrangler...

Now as many know Lupin arrived and then turned into demon Lupin through her phantom pregnancy.... turning a once peaceful Poodle Central into "Poodle run for your lives Central"

Well today my girls have chosen to sit together in one of the nests

Snuggled up together
And it warms my heart ♥🐾🐾
So here they are
Daisy and Lupin who chose to sit together

CHAPTER 56

Good Evening from Poodle Central....

Daisy went swimming today ...and Lupin got chucked in the bath cause I said she was looking raggedy ...

We'll have no fear...

Daisy all fluffed and blowed 👍🏻🖤

And Lupin?

She's now rocking a 70's disco fluff 🙄🙄

I said dang Lupin you're rocking that bouffant 💇
Her hairs grown like wild fire

CHAPTER 57

Teddy says he knows his mum loves him ....

Cause she went out in the cold and rain to get the poodle hordes Sunday treat ...

Custard Slices

There will be some happy sighs tomorrow

CHAPTER 58

I'm still running behind from Christmas

Well finally Lupin is modelling her "gnome hoody"

Designer made by her Auntie Beth and Auntie Stevie
She is now officially "arrived"

I'll try and take some better photos tomorrow- as the gang have had their faces shaved now too (as I decided Daisy was turning into hairy Daisy lol)

Alfie is missing from the line up- why? You ask

Well Alfie had a mishap in his hoody and it had to be washed and dried

He'll be modelling tomorrow

CHAPTER 59

Good Evening from Poodle Central.....

The Lupini strikes again....

She managed to get hold of my "Belle" poodle I had made (I had a Daisy one done too)

Well sadly Boo is now a straggled Boo 😿

No shouting or chastising here though, all Lupin sees is a new toy 🧸

God love Lupin, she's definitely been sent to keep me on my toes and eyes in the back of my head

Now remember Poodle Wrangling isn't all easy sailing .... but also remember anything worth having isn't straight forward

And Lupin did come and give me some loving Butter wouldn't melt 🖤

CHAPTER 60

Ssssssssshhh......

All that can be heard at Poodle Central is snoring......

Well aside from the scowling Daisy has thrown at me at being chucked in the bath for some swimming....

Alfie, Teddy and Lupin are having 40 winks so I'm using this opportunity to get the stuffies off the window sill and start "stuffy surgery"
Gnome
Lamb Chop
Daisy's bear (don't ask)

Now If I can just tip toe back to the toy box with them without being seen

CHAPTER 61

After a day of mischief (a long day if your called Lupin) .... all the little Parkinson's are Knick knack knackered....

Gnome is breathing a sigh of relief, he's still got his innards

And the Lupini is dreaming of chasing squirrels 🐿
Teddy is having 40 winks and worrying Miss Snakey will be sewn soon after having her squeak removed - Lupin style

Alfie is wondering when Miss Snakey 🐍 arrived and what the heck is Teddy doing with all those snakeys 🐍
And Daisy???

Well, it's hard being ruler of the universe when you've a noisy big little sister interrupting your important power naps

CHAPTER 62

Teddy's put paw to paper to celebrate this day of loving ....

I'm a loving little Teddy, I like to shake my bum

I've plenty of time for loving, and playing kiss and run
 So, if you want a gentleman, who can shower you in treats

Text XOXO and we'll do a post covid meet

Love Teddy

Big kisses to Sara Bullock 🖤🖤
Big kisses to Belle Gracie 🖤🖤

In fact, Teddy says big kisses to all the girls today! 🖤🖤🖤

CHAPTER 63

The gang have had breakfast

And today's serenade for Daisy?
Sam Cook - twisting the night away

And Yes....we're now sporting 2 corns

CHAPTER 64

Lupini V the squeaky ball

Lupini - 1
Ball – 0

Tonight's entertainment
Lupin style ...

Dissecting the orange
squeaky ball 😈😈😈

CHAPTER 65

Good Morning from Poodle Central....

As you can see the hurricane that was Lupini has been in the lounge...shredding the junk mail

Daisy put her paw down and sent the bouncing Lupin (and Teddy) to the park with their Dad

And now Daisy is inspecting the aftermath of the Lupin's handiwork

Daisy says she will go for a stroll when they come back from the park, but until then her and Alfie are enjoying the quiet...

The moral...?

never turn your back on a Lupin and if she's quiet, panic!

<u>CHAPTER 66</u>

Lupini V Bath Bubbles

Lupin - 1
Bath bubbles and Me – 0

Quiet bath times have ended...

No longer can I sneak off to be lazy and read my book

No, Lupin has decided I had a choice...

Either give her the bubbles or she was jumping in to get them herself 😕🙀🙀

CHAPTER 67

Good Evening from Poodle Central....

This week has had its own dramas, which will remain at Poodle Central...

Daisy just rolled her eyes

However today 3 of the little Parkinson's were at the back door ▌checking on their Dad's progress at staining the back garden fence

Miss Lupin is now rocking two colour flashes ...we have no idea where her hair is going to settle 😶

There's brown on the bottom of her ears

CHAPTER 68

Miss Daisy coming downstairs from her swim....

And seeing the chaos left by the Lupinicaine 🙄

Alfie was unavailable for comment

Teddy says he was in his hole and saw nothing

CHAPTER 69

Good Morning from Poodle Central....

Daisy here...

I thought somebody best do an update and Alfie and Teddy are no writers so La! La! you've got me, Daisy

What about the Lupini I hear you ask?

Well, it's often like wacky races around here with my mum checking what Lupin is up to - so you've no chance that Lupin is going to stop her mischief to write - Lupin says that's far too boring!

So, a snakey run broke out this morning and ended with a battering

Yes, I did roll my eyes

Lupin managed to get Miss Snakey 🍃which Teddy was not fussed about ...

Now the Lupini isn't daft, after dragging Miss Snakey about for a little while and getting no rise from the Tedster she realised Miss Snakey 🍃wasn't worth grabbing 😕

So, que a prancing Lupin trying to grab Snakey 🍃

Now I will add here, that Lupin is no little dot 🌑and she's no limbo Lupin either!

So, she's not worked out how to approach Teddy's hole let alone try and get in

Both myself and Alfie found this highly entertaining watching Lupin look for a Lupin sized entrance
Teddy scowling

Well, there was no way - So eventually Lupin came back on the bed and sat with Me and Alfie,

Commiserating with Miss Snakey , who incidentally is missing some of tail (yes Lupin's handiwork)

Mum then shouted it was pee pee time, so begrudgingly I got up

Teddy and Alfie ran down the stairs and Lupin saw her chance!

Even my mum looked!

A Lupin on her belly grabbed Snakeys tongue and dragged him out of Teddy's hole!

Well, we got a photo of her with her prize - just before Teddy arrived back upstairs and promptly grabbed snakey back and gave a growl to Lupin, which turned into a scrag as the daft Lupin thought it was a love growl!

So, it's only 9.30am and as you can see it's any wonder, I manage to get any kip around here with these muppets!

After all I am Daisy - ruler of the universe

CHAPTER 70

Breaking News at Poodle Central....

Lupin has gone from woolly Lupin to Pretty Lupin

More photos to follow of the gang

CHAPTER 71

It's a Poodle Central photo shoot!

We've no more unruly woolly poodles!
Alfie said he was far too tired to participate 😔
Daisy actually had her spa day last week ... (well ruler of the universe does have some perks she says 😊)

Lupin has found her big girl hair cut

And Teddy says look at my ears!

CHAPTER 72

Please send positive vibes to Miss Lupin she's currently admitted to the vets

Lupin has been off all day and not eating or drinking (she was fine yesterday)

She's vomited blood-tinged liquid and running a temp and dehydrated
Kind thoughts would be appreciated

The vets are rehydrating, doing bloods, X-rays and scans
🖤
The gang are missing their sis

CHAPTER 73

Update on Lupin…

The vets have just called
Lupin has had a settled night,

She was very dehydrated and has now had fluids,
bloods, anti-nausea drugs, drugs to protect her
tummy and for pain relief some opioids

The nurse did say Lupin woke at 3am and wanted
entertaining (me that's her usual time)

Today they are scanning and doing the X-rays to
rule out she's nothing stuck or blocking anywhere

They will call again later today
All is quiet at Poodle Central….

Even Daisy says it's quiet

Thank you everyone
for your kind words 🖤
Hopefully the Lupini
will be home soon x

<u>CHAPTER 74</u>

Lupini Update ......

I've spoken to nurse and vet and there's good new re scan and X-ray

Neither revealed any foreign body or blocks But Lupin's lymph nodes and her tummy are inflamed leading the vet to infection

Lupin is bright (never tell her while she was sedated the vets did a rectal exam too ☻) but still on the drip

She is starting to drink but refusing food

Continuing with the meds and she is stopping in tonight and the vets are going to try with some food later

They will telephone us between 7/8 in the morning with an update

Thank you everyone for your support for us 🐾🐾 🐾💜

CHAPTER 75

Good Afternoon from Poodle Central....

Now some folk might think Poodle Wrangling is all smiles and whoops ....

However, they haven't met my 4

After the high drama of Miss Lupin being carted off to the in patients at the vets, last night we hoped for a quiet night (well aside from Lupin's wind)

Sadly, yet again I was wrong....
Everyone had their last pee pee's and trotted to bed...

Ok

First up Daisy, with a love swipe across my kisser
Ok I'm coming

Up I get (Daisy no longer jumps on or off the bed as sometimes she doesn't land like a gymnast)

Takes her for a pee pee
Back in bed
Not 5 minutes later .... swipe

What!!!
Daisy now decides she wants a drink
Ok up I get

Daisy had a drink
Back in bed
Rustling on bed

Teddy stood wanting quilt to be lifted
Fine ....

All settle again
Lupin arrives, sits on top of me

Que a bit of early morning stroking and loving
Ok
All settles again

Up gets Alfie
For the love of God!
Alfie going for a drink

He has his drink
Me? Where is he?

Ok up again off in search of Alf
Grabs Alfie, chucks him back on the bed
Ok all settle

Daisy looks at me
Don't even think about it!

So, after 1 Lupin loving time, 4 Daisy trips, 2 Alfie
trips and numerous quilt lifting for Teddy

Up gets Neil for work
Yeah!... let's have an hour

Oh no not a chance
What's next you ask? well 7.40am the window
cleaner arrived 😩😩😩

So up we got

The Lupini is feeling much better as you can see

However Tracy after we spent all that time growing her she is now sporting a bald leg and pom 🙈🙈🙈

Sue and Beth said shave the other leg, she'll have a matching pair 🙈🙈

Is it Nap time????😴😴😴😴

CHAPTER 76

Well, no one ever said Poodle Wrangling was all fun
And Miss Lupin has certainly arrived at Poodle Central with a bang!

First the poor little girl had to endure a phantom pregnancy (sorry Daisy's just informed me it was actually Her, Alfie and Teddy that endured the mad Lupini 😳)

And then at weekend she was admitted to the vets with blood in her vomit

Well, she went back yesterday with blood in her poop 💩

And now we are waiting for the scan results of her pancreas etc

It's all on the chin here at Poodle Central, we take the knocks (and the odd shaved legs Lupin 😕) and move forward

Daisy has taken up residence in the nest in the living room favoured by Lupin at night sometimes

Teddy is mounting a window lookout
And Alfie? he says Lupin? who the hell is Lupin? 😜

*********Update...*********

Pippa the vet just called
The scan has shown slight changes to her pancreas
So, they are confident with the blood results that Lupin has pancreatitis

They are continuing the meds
Lupin has eaten some chicken today

They are keeping her in for at least another 24 hrs
and will reassess tomorrow

Hoping she continues to eat and is bright
I asked the question re Addison's and Lupin's
blood work has shown none of the flags either on
Friday or last night

So, with the scan showing pancreatic changes
they are confident Addison's is not in the picture
Bloods will be repeated tomorrow

The cause?...
They say in many many cases it's never known
what triggered an incident

When she comes home it's 8 weeks of bland food
so tonight at poodle central Daisy, Teddy and Alfie
get to choose their favourites as they've 8 weeks of
bland food too in support of the Lupini 😊

CHAPTER 77

It's Bo Bo time at Poodle Central...

And Miss Daisy May is getting comfy ...

CHAPTER 78

Good Morning from the Lupini

Lupin says "Daisy hasn't stopped laughing since I came home! she's finding my lob sided poms hilarious...

personally, I think she should mind her own business and give me some sympathy, as I've a chunk missing off my belly too!

I've a whole heap of meds and I'm having little meals now

Sigh....my mum keeps looking at these poms ... Tracy what should she do with them???

CHAPTER 79

I've been searching ages for some Bluebells

And finally got them yesterday

So, planting today

CHAPTER 80

Daisy was caught with her tongue out today ...

But she knew something was happening behind her 😳😃

A flash of Lupin dragging *Miss Snakey* back up the stairs....

Lupin hasn't got the hang of snakeynapping 😔😔

Teddy didn't bat an eyelid; he's not fussed as long as it's not *snakey*

CHAPTER 81

Good Afternoon from Poodle Central......

It's been a little quiet on the shenanigans front here, with Lupin being poorly and the new grass being laid

However (rolls eyes) it changed today

I was minding my own business wiping the kitchen worktops when out of the corner of my eye I saw a beige flash out the back door....

Hmm I thought, no idea what the is???
Can't be a poodle
Can't be a snakey
Certainly not a Neil

So, I put my cloth down and walked to the back door where a crowd had gathered ...ok by crowd I mean Daisy, Alfie and Tedd's

All watching Lupin running around the garden dragging one of my bath towels in mouth!

Now as I stood there thinking - no apparently, I haven't seen it all

I managed to regain my voice and shout "Lupin! bring that towel back in"

Crowd watching
Me steps outside

"C'mon here!" Sets off towards Lupin
And we're off!

The daft Lupini thinks I'm joining in the fun and ups her game, ducking and weaving, dragging my beige towel around a bush
Me chasing

Finally, off she runs inside and straight up the stairs back to the bathroom where I found her (when I caught up) happily chewing on my towel 😕😕😕😕
Me?

"It will have to go in the washer now"

Lupin as I'm taking her new prized possession "are you crazy?!?!"

So, as I marched downstairs (the crowd had gathered at the bottom of the stairs)
A sulking Lupin walked past Daisy, Alfie and Teddy

And dramatically threw herself in her nest
The boys realising the action had finished went back to the living room

Daisy?????
I swear if she could have, she'd have popped her paw on her face and uttered "why me?"

The moral???

Buy Lupin her own towel 😂😂😂

CHAPTER 82

Good morning from Poodle Central...,

Now when I last glimpsed the poodle horde, they were sending the *zzzzzz* as the photo shows of Miss Daisy and Miss Lupin

All was quiet 😶

However, my mistake was smiling and rolling over to have a cheeky half hour *zzzzz*
I awoke to snorting!
And I mean piggy snorting

Looks on bed .... everyone's accounted for except???
Did you guess???

Yes ... the Lupini
Sigh.... ok what's she up to
I'm wide awake here now!
Still hearing the snorting and nails against a hard surface

Follows the noise
And ta! da!

There's one Lupin in the bath with her nose in the plug hole sniffing and snorting!

Now Lupin is obsessed with the bath at the best of times and always wants to jump in - water or no water

Hence if I want a quiet bath there's no Lupins allowed

However today Lupin found a new entertainment-snorting the bathroom plug
And I mean snorting 👃👃

Me "what are you doing?"
Lupin "checking the plumbing"

Me "go and find a stuffy, there's plenty to play with"

Lupin throwing a filthy look "you spoil all my fun"

Now it's quite possible I have the first poodle plumber ever, however it's not activity I'm going to encourage otherwise I can imagine using the bathroom in the middle of the night and Lupin will be doing a "plug hole inspection!" 👃👃👃

The moral???

Oh, why couldn't my heart have been stolen by a goldfish instead of these loopy poodles 😄😄😄

CHAPTER 83

Good Evening from Poodle Central....

It was high drama earlier this evening and my
poor heart took a jolt...

Neil had gone taking the bins out - shutting the
gates behind him
And we went about getting dinner ready
Roll call!

Lupin comes a running
Daisy and Alfie present and correct

Tedd's??
Ted??

He must be in his hole says Neil - I'll pop it under
All meals eaten

Neil- Teddy hasn't eaten his dinner
Me-???
Neil - Teddy isn't in his hole

Me- 👻👻👻full blown panic
Now remember there's a 3-gate lock 🔒
So, Teddy can't have gone walkabout

Me- 👻👻👻👻headless chicken
Neil checks upstairs
No Tedd's
Teddy isn't downstairs
The garden looks empty

Me- 👻👻👻👻👻
Neil- goes into garden looking in bushes

And Ta! Da!

One Teddy is found, mooching around enjoying himself

Me - flat lined 😰😰😰

Teddy strolls back indoors - what???
Me - 🙀🙀

Now the moral- don't go into hyperdrive when you know the Tedster can't have gone anywhere, the 3 lock gates work

CHAPTER 84

Sometimes we find special friends in unexpected places...

In a poodle group years ago a gang of ladies laughed and shared their love of poodles ...

Fast forward quite a few years and both Me and Neil, Daisy, Alfie, Teddy & Lupin are very lucky to have Beth, Stevie, Bubby, Sassy and MJ as our friends

Today a beautiful bouquet of flowers  arrived
Addressed to Daisy who's been unwell recently
And even the wrapping had Daisy's on

Love You guys 🖤

CHAPTER 85

Breaking News from Poodle Central!!

You find us here on this sunny Sunday morning with high drama ...

As I've previously said, stealth is not in the Lupini's vocabulary...but God love her she tries 😃

Any way this morning as Teddy was sat in the suitcase in the bathroom (I was making the beds)

Lupin decided she needed her bunny 🐰

Now Teddy has never been fussed about bunny, as bunny isn't a hedgehog 🦔or snakey 🐍

But suddenly bunny looked a whole lot more desirable when he saw Lupin wanted bunny 😊

Queue Lupin trying to drag bunny out - nope, no way was Teddy letting bunny go

Lupin shifting towards bunny with a quick tug on his leg- nope, Teddy I swear had a smile on his face by now

Lupin moaning - she tried the sympathy vote - nope Teddy definitely enjoying himself now

This could have been part pay back for Lupin running with Teddy's red loving hedgehog 🦔into the garden the other day

Teddy was most put out he had to go save hedgy Anyways as you can see from the quickly snapped photos - Teddy was having fun

Lupin???...not so much

So much so she decided to abandon bunny 🐰(
Daisy told her get back in there!)

And go for a quick chew on my bath math 😶😶
And the end???

Teddy has now taken bunny 🐰to his hole 😈😈😈
So, it's game on!

Will the Lupin rescue bunny? will bunny 🐰now
live with snakey 🐍
I've no idea???

But Teddy's hole is getting like a zoo under there!
😈😈😈😈

CHAPTER 86

Breaking News from Poodle Central!

Bunny was liberated!!

The Lupin in a full-on assault grabbed bunny and starting running (Yep, the Lupini has worked it out you need to grab and run 🤏😄)

Teddy was taken aback!
He had only just got upstairs for a stuffy check and Lupin dived...catching the little lothario mid hedgy loving

Off she ran and straight out the back door!
Now at this point the Tedster is right behind her and Me, Daisy and Alfie had side stepped to avoid this unfolding train wreck 🙀

Now this is where the Lupini needs to up her game .... she completely forgot about bunny and decided a game of chase was much more fun!

So, bunny was
abandoned while the Tedster and Lupini ran full speed around the water fountain

On the upside?
Bunny had a very nice sunbathe while this was going on and a nice bit of "bunny time" 😎🐰

But I can assure you he was promptly escorted by Teddy back upstairs to his hole where I'm told bunny is regaling Snakey 🐍about his trip 😎😎

CHAPTER 87

Good Morning from Poodle Central....

Ok it's official I'm in the dog house!
Why you cry???

Well, the Tedster aka Mr sometimes potato 🥔ear struck again

He's not normally good at hiding when his ear gets mucky - remember the Tedster is a sensitive little soul

But he had
So today when I was having my morning cup of tea ☕ I casually spotted his ear as his flap was back at bit

Me... is that wax?
Teddy... rolls eyes
Me... c'mon bring your body over here

Teddy .... not on your life, heading for his hole
Poodle audience of Daisy, Alfie and Lupin watching

Me grabs the Teddy
And is rewarded with a scowl
Me... right let's go clean that ear
Teddy .... dying swan

So off we trot, well I trot, Teddy is tucked under my arm

And Teddy watches as I get the ear stuff out
And as I go near, lift the flap, about to put cleaner in

The scream!!

Jeez, Teddy, I've not touched you yet!

Teddy.... ok sorry I peeked too soon, try it again
So, I go again
Ear cleaner in
Teddy screams 😵😵

Anyway, a good cleaning later and I can assure
you no Teddy's were harmed during the wax
cleaning

Teddy marches away from me without a backward
glance!

At present he is sun bathing on the window sill
and completely ignoring me!

Ah well.... can't win em all

Time for another cup of tea ☕ me thinks

CHAPTER 88

Good Morning from Poodle Central....

Daisy is strolling around with a big smile on her face this morning.

Why you ask???

Well Alfie, Teddy and Lupin are off to be beautified today by Tracy and she gets the run of the place without them!

Daisy went last week to be beautified and had a lovely time and now today she's looking forward to her day of chilling

(Quiet whooping from Daisy) 😊

Of course, she has yet to tell the threesome they are off to the hairdressers and she's looking forward to that too!
Daisy says today is a good day 💇😊🖤

CHAPTER 89

Good Afternoon from Poodle Central....

Daisy said she's had a secret ALL day!

Alfie, Teddy and Lupin have been to be beautified.... yes, that's true

But the Lupini has had a makeover!

Well Daisy says she was sick of looking at odd Lupini so said "give her poms!"

Alfie and Teddy look very very handsome too!

CHAPTER 90

Just had a lovely visit from Susan

Enjoyed a chat in the garden and the Lupini made a new best friend

Teddy enjoyed a bit of loving
Miss Snakey enjoyed her garden time
Bunny still hasn't been liberated

Alfie was shy 🛖

And Daisy?.... well Daisy said all this was not interesting to her at all 😀

Thank you for the donations, Susan and telling Neil "Your owt!"
Xx

CHAPTER 91

This weather best go do one!

My poor Daisy needed anchoring this morning, she was being lifted off the ground!

Daisy says this is no way acceptable, as "rulers of the universe" are not supposed to "fly"

Lupin just stood opened mouthed

Daisy (and Lupin) are sporting new hoodies
Saying cutie patootie 🖤(Lupin isn't wearing hers yet)

And in breaking news!
Bunny has been liberated!!!

He is currently abandoned in the living room, Daisy went inspecting ...

Lupin lost interest as Teddy just glanced as she pranced past with 🐰bunny

Pssst...Lupin, be careful Teddy is playing a game.... watch out bunny will suddenly disappear 👀

CHAPTER 92

Good Morning from Poodle Central....

Lupin is in the dog house...

Why come the cries from the "Lupini brigade!"

Well yesterday she was on hyper power and accidentally got too rough with the Tedster when they were scragging ...

And as Susan can attest, she was on full "toddler show off" when she came to visit, running around and wanting to play with a slightly miffed Teddy

Well, this morning Lupin decided she would go liberate Bunny 🐰from the Tedsters hole 🐹

Now there's no stealth from the Lupin - what you see is what you get

And what Teddy saw was a great big Lupin kisser coming into his hole!

Que a scream!

Now as far as Lupin is concerned yesterday's shenanigans are yesterday and Teddy's bruised ego needs to suck it up...

Not so with Teddy!

He sees a black demon about to breech his hole Anyways...the screaming stopped the Lupin in her tracks and she sat miffed, outside Teddy's hole wondering what the fuss was about

Teddy?

Well, he marched out of his hole, with not a glance at Lupin and jumped on the bed

Lupin - what????

Me - you've upset him

Lupin??

Me- you'll have to wait now until he wants to play
Lupin- oh for the love of God!

Alfie?...pretending he's asleep, this is not his circus and not his monkeys- besides he's quite comfy and doesn't want to be a Teddy stand in

Daisy?.... looks at me and her face said it all "See?!?!?!"

So, as I finish my cup of tea - in peace-

All I hear is a skulking Lupin looking for mischief....
Sigh....

Ok I'm up 😄😄😄

CHAPTER 93

Breaking news from Poodle Central!!!

We've had a "Peepacide!"

Currently investigations are ongoing ....

No one is admitting to this horrendous attack on Yellow Peep ....

Although Daisy has been seen next to a banner saying "blame the Lupini one!" 😄😶

Investigations will continue, however catching the culprit will be difficult as apparently there were no witnesses ....
Randy Rooster (who mysteriously has been given respite in scragging) is claiming he "saw nothing "

CHAPTER 94

A whodunnit poodle central update!

No further evidence has been discovered today via poop 💩 inspection 😱

So, Randy Rooster was cornered and interviewed....

However, the rooster clammed up whilst eating a suspicious 😠 slice of pizza 🍕 he claims he found...

Daisy noted that the Lupini had been seen earlier throwing said pizza 🍕 around, claiming the rooster had been "bribed"

Randy shuffled off - claiming he wanted a lawyer

Teddy and Alfie were unavailable for comment as they were both sunbathing in the teatime sun on Teddy's sofa

Daisy was busy having her face shaved
And Lupin???.... well Lupin had declared she was tired and withdrew to her nest for 40 winks

The plot thickens

CHAPTER 95

Breaking Whodunnit news from Poodle Central......

There has still been no sign of the infamous missing ear off yellow peep and poop analysis is showing clear....

Teddy and Alfie are mystified why anyone would want to harm yellow peep and watching events carefully
Lupin says this is all very worrying as the finger keeps getting pointed at her ...

And Daisy????.... well, the intrepid ruler of the universe caught these top-secret photos last night and is sure there's more to Randy Rooster than he is admitting

He can be clearly shown having a meeting with the Hedgehog 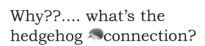mafia and entertaining them!

Why??.... what's the hedgehog connection?

Apparently, Randy thought the meeting went well although it seems he doesn't hold his sambuca drinking as seen in Daisy's photos...

Is Randy a lush?

What are the hedgehogs doing?
Does Teddy know his hedgehogs are out??

Does Lupin know there's been a gathering of stuffies and she wasn't invited???

And Alfie???...mild mannered Alfie just keeping out of view???

It's all very suspicious...and Randy needs 2 paracetamols 😊 😊

<u>CHAPTER 96</u>

It's a whodunnit update from Poodle Central....

Randy the Rooster has come clean!!

He's told his sorry tale over some Coca Cola (other soft drinks are available and nice too ☺) after he sobered up from his Sambuca binge

Now....

Did you figure out the plot???

We know the Lupini ate yellow peeps ear ...but why???

Normally the Lupini likes Squeakies...so it's out of character for her ...

So, what could have convinced her to chew the ear??
And why???

The conclusion will be told later today....

CHAPTER 97

Good Afternoon from Poodle Central....

Did you guess???

Ok in order to figure out this tangled web we need to look back a few days....

Remember when Teddy and Lupin were playing and Lupin got a little rough and made Teddy scream?

Well, someone was watching....
And someone wanted payback ...
Who you cry??

Well, it was Teddy's original red hedgehog 🦔, hedgy hated seeing his beloved Teddy screaming

So, he hatched a plan

First, he went to snakey 🐍 and asked for help in framing the Lupini ...

So Snakey contacted the hedgehog 🦔 mafia who then employed Randy the Rooster to shimmy up to Lupin whispering sweet nothings ......

A pact was formed 🦔🐍🦔🦔🦔🦔🐓
A plan was made

Randy would encourage Lupin to nibble yellow peep and do a quick runner.... leaving no evidence behind

Lupin would be the prime suspect and peepless cause yellow squeaky peep would get taken off her.... causing her much irritation

All the while red hedgy would be smiling at payback

Lupin is currently searching for Randy the Rooster .... with mischief on her mind!

And snakey is in Tedd's hole watching the events

The whereabouts of the hedgehog mafia is currently unknown; however, it is believed they have moved into Rooster smuggling...

Alfie says this espionage is all too much and is thankful his gnome likes a quiet life like him

Daisy is particularly impressed by her photographic skills this week ....and caught the threesome making their plans of mischief- she thinks she might continue with her awesome skills

And Teddy???...in his public statement he says he is shocked by his beloved
hedgehogs , but in
private he is giving each
and every one an extra
special hug

CHAPTER 98

A Poodle Central Update....

Poor Randy was cornered by the Lupini and she took him out into the wet garden where she promptly abandoned him!

A smile on her face as she ran back inside
I went and got the hapless Rooster and brought him back in

But he's started his
Saturday night
shenanigans early
....

He's back on the bottle and added nuts 🥜 as an accompaniment

Me thinks Teddy needs to come and have a word with him

CHAPTER 99

Good Afternoon from Poodle Central....

It's Daisy here,

I've been swimming today and now feel all refreshed and blow dried ...

Apparently when I'm swimming the Lupini feels the need to sit and watch and give score marks on my doggy paddling 😊🐕

I told her she wouldn't be as quick to hold those score cards up if she was the one swimming...

Any ways my mum finally found the cause of my being "off" she took me to the vets again and yes right at the back of my mouth hiding was a grizzly looking molar that is bleeding 😠

So, after much chatting with the vets ...they are bringing in a specialist anaesthetist and they are going in and quick and whipping that tooth out

Now me I was like????

But my mum says I can't have that sore tooth in my mouth as it will only get worse
Me????

I'm going for a full check over bloods, heart etc (even though I told them rulers of the universe are indestructible)

And one of my regular vets (Lori) is going to be with me

I'm slightly concerned .... I'll only have 6 teeth left but hey ho as long as I can eat my duckie whirls then all is good

So, for your pleasure...

Me Daisy, ruler of the universe modelling in the garden  after swimming

CHAPTER 100

It's Friday and the rooster is sloshed......

<u>CHAPTER 101</u>

Good Evening from Poodle Central......

Daisy is gutted....
All week I promised her a Kentucky chicken this weekend ...

Her ultimate favourite!
And wham! today as we get up Lupin has a "popping" belly

Daisy "phht!"

I said to Daisy we can't have a Kentucky with Lupin's belly off Daisy "she can have a piece of cod out of the freezer"

I said Daisy we can't do that, remember we all have it or none of us have it

Daisy "I'm sick of living in this democracy, you lot get what you want .... get me my Kentucky"

I said Daisy we can have it next Saturday
Daisy "are you for real!!"
I said I'll put some thighs in and you can all have plain nice chicken

Daisy....marches off to her hole

Sigh....you can't please em all

CHAPTER 102

Neil!!
You better come get Randy!
He's been at my wine!

CHAPTER 103

Teddy has a visitor on his sofa......

Randy is catching some rays 🌕
Ah well at least he hasn't a drink 🥛in his hand 😃

CHAPTER 104

Ahhh Randy ......

You knew it was coming, payback for getting involved in the hedgehog 🦔mafia Lupini plot...

Randy's sunbathing was rudely interrupted by a Lupini scragging 😜😀

Will the hedgehogs 🦔🦔🦔🦔🦔retaliate???

CHAPTER 105

Hot news from Poodle Central......

The hedgehog mafia is back and showing their displeasure at Randy being straggled!

It was an ambush!

And Teddy couldn't contain his laughter at the poor Lupini

She was going for a quiet bath after Daisy had been swimming and bamm!

What greeted her was a hedgehog delegation!

Lupini was not amused and now says all those hedgehogs best watch out as this is war!!!

And to add insult to injury Teddy was holding Miss Snakey ransom!

Randy the rooster was not available for comment Alfie said he only came upstairs for a kip

And Daisy said ...for god's sake! the stuffies are running amok!

CHAPTER 106

Good afternoon from Poodle Central....

Daisy here - I've been snapping photos again as I've decided I'm a very good photographer...oh and modest ...

Alfie is snuggling with his gnome on the sofa
Teddy is having a bit of hedgehog loving

So that left the Lupini
Well, I caught her!
She gave a right royal scragging to rabbit (who Teddy had brought down to see the sun) and Randy (who was in the wrong place at the wrong time)

Anyways she straggled them in the front window!! Rabbit and Randy are currently recovering and no seams were spilt during this stuffy attack Lupin is now having 40 winks

And my Mum?
Well as I saw pie was on the menu I requested "mini meat" for tea - that's Turkey mince to you lot!
Well, I'll keep patrolling and see if there's any more snaps to be had
Daisy xx

CHAPTER 107

Good Afternoon from Poodle Central...

It's been a busy morning here with friends arriving on their way to their long-awaited holidays...

All poodles were up and counted...well aside from Daisy who declared it was "too" early to be up and wanted picky up

Jacqueline, Olga, Pronto and Eimear arrived with the table for the auction (and a table which she made for us last year which is so unusual) and much to Lupini's delight stuffies!

Teddy kept a close eye on the stuffies, which Lupin had decided were in fact all hers

Now we've never had a crocodile 🐊at poodle central .... It was such a pretty crock

However, the Lupini decided what crock actually needed was a foot redoing and destuffing 🐊💀

Lupini - 1
Crock – 0

Teddy has since silently snook off with pink bunny 🐰up to his hole ⬤

Now Alfie found himself a friend ...Eimear was a snuggle bunny and decided

Alfie's cushion looked comfy so she and Alfie took an after-breakfast nap
Pronto kept watch on the proceedings from near his mum Jacqueline- then going for a snuggle off mum Olga

And we've soda bread!

We're looking forward to trying it with bacon

Lupin did decide she was packing her bag and going on holiday with Jacqueline and Olga....and was mighty "put out" that we told her she couldn't go –

queue the screaming!

A lovely morning was had

Enjoy your
holidays
everyone!

CHAPTER 108

Daisy had her pre dental check today and marched out of the vets with a smile on her face ......

Her tooth is actually not as grizzly

So, the vets are giving antibiotics to see if we can avoid the extraction

Daisy is well in herself (well aside from the other morning when I got her out of bed early, it was all grumpy Daisy 😊)

She's eating and as you all can see enjoying the sunshine ⚪
Daisy says it feels like a "Kentucky Weekend!"

CHAPTER 109

Good Morning from A bleary eyed Poodle Central....

Well apparently, the neighbours enjoying the nice weather prompted Lupin into security mode 😕

So, at 2.20am (I kid you not) the Lupini after hearing the neighbours (who were in their back garden 🍄 chatting, I will add not loudly)

She broke into "Charge of the light brigade Lupini!"

Running down the stairs on full volume "I'll protect you mum!"

😦😦😦
Lupin!
Bed!

A rather "put out" Lupin shuffled back
Ok 😴😴😴
And ta! da!

4.30am Lupin heard suspicious 😮 sounds,
Go back to sleep Lupin

It's the other neighbours and their hot tub
Lupin...are you crazy! we're under attack!
It could be aliens

Me...as long as they don't take my kettle all is well...
Lupin ...staring
And she's off!

Neil let's her out - she might want a wee
No...
What she wanted was to ensure the estate knew
she was here and ready! 😑😑

Drags Lupin back in

Daisy lifts her head as the
Lupin flops next to her-
don't bring your crazy here
Loop

So, all settled...eventually

And now as you can see the
little Parkinson's are having
a snooze

With Lupin lifting her head and looking at me
"what??"
Sigh....

Cup of tea ☕

<u>CHAPTER 110</u>

When you're enjoying the quiet ....

Before your sister and brother come back from the park....

Daisy May 🖤

CHAPTER 111

Please if you can spare kind thoughts today

Daisy ruler of the universe is unwell ...

No Kentucky was had at poodle central last night as Daisy suffered a neurological incident ...

She was extremely unsettled last night and at some point, I think her sight was affected,

She's calmed this morning but we are off to the vets at 12.30 as she is not drinking

CHAPTER 112

Scooby has fallen ...

CHAPTER 113

We are heartbroken at Poodle Central

Today my absolute world shattered...

My sidekick, my soul mate, my love has departed

I never got to see my beautiful Daisy enter the world but I promised her she would never leave it without me by her side

Daisy had the heart of a lion and a will of steel she was my beautiful dot whom I adored utterly

I remember picking her up and my heart sang and throughout our journey together she has given nothing but love and joy

For anyone who ever met Daisy they knew she was a teeny weeny but tough

She met many of our poodle friends and in typical Daisy ruler of the universe style nodded and marched on by

I thought that fate was cruel taking our beautiful

Belle only months ago but fate has now stolen
both my beautiful girls and I'm just beyond words

Run free my darling
you have my heart
💜 always

CHAPTER 114

Daisy *"ruler of the universe"* has been laid to rest

She was buried under the laurel archway next to the Queen

And has her own personal guard of honour

A Daisy plant is arriving tomorrow to go at the side

Lupin and Alfie watched from the side-lines Teddy said goodbye indoors

Run free my heart 🖤

CHAPTER 115

Everyone knows Teddy is the thinker of the family...

He wouldn't come outside yesterday to see Daisy laid to rest. But that's ok,

He thinks and then decides

So today as I'm looking for him, I see this

Teddy had gone and sat on the lawn near to Daisy

He was out there a good hour

CHAPTER 116

It's a story which has to be told ...as Daisy would
have rolled her eyes at it

We are all sat in the garden today
Some in the shade
Some near to Daisy

And Lupin? well scratching feverishly at the
fence...

Come sit down Lupin
Nope
More fence scratching

Ok I get up thinking one of her toys has got stuck
No nothing

Lupin still scratching at the fence
Then I spy through the fence what she sees

A tennis 🎾ball...
And she wants it ...

I try giving her her own 🎾tennis ball ...

No
She wants what she can't have

And here my friends is where Daisy would have
rolled her eyes...

I got up

Goes up the side of the house, through the 3 gates
and knocks on next doors front door

Vivienne, please may I buy that tennis ball in your back garden?

Lupin has seen it and wants it
Oh, she can have it says Vivienne

So, I wander back ... said tennis ball in hand and as you can see, she's rather pleased with herself

CHAPTER 117

Can I just say a big heart felt thank you to everyone who took time to say kind words for Daisy ....

Daisy walked to the beat of her own drum and her little shadow cast a long way, I was incredibly privileged to love her

Thank you to everyone for the cards, flowers, and gifts remembering Daisy 🖤

Her Daisy sun catcher is hanging as it should over her

CHAPTER 118

It was very warm today....

Teddy decided his spot for today was next to the Daisy plant 🖤

Cooling down was in order, so their dad went and got mini plain McFlurrys for them

Que ice cream 🍦 in the garden

CHAPTER 119

A week ago today my world was ripped apart,

Daisy made her trip across the bridge and left me broken hearted ....

Today around the same time I was saying a final goodbye to my little girl last week, her plot is all finished...

Perfect for Daisy ruler of the universe

Today is a sad day because Daisy isn't here but also because today would have been Belle's 5th Birthday...
Our little miracle

But I know both my girls are together and if Belle has her way, she will be making Daisy roll her eyes on overtime

Obviously, there will be an abundance of Snakeys and Kentucky chicken

Miss you Scooby

Happy Birthday
Boo

CHAPTER 120

Now the other day I noticed Lupin had left a squeaky ball near Daisy's plot

I just went and picked it up and handed it back to Lupin

Well yesterday twice she did the same - took a ball to Daisy and dropped it in front of her

Again, I picked it up and gave it back to Lupin Even saying "Lupin I don't think Daisy wants your ball, she wasn't fussed about it"

Well today Lupin has taken squeaky hedgehog and left it in front of Daisy

And I'll leave it this time.... why?

Well Lupin is obviously telling me something, Squeakies are her most prized possessions and if she's taking them to Daisy, she has a reason

So, I'll let Lupin decide

CHAPTER 121

You know when you come downstairs and there's a paddling pool in your living room that you live with poodles ......

It is, I stress going outside, Neil just inflated indoors 🙁

Neil's got the gang a paddling pool so they can keep cool...

But Teddy says he preferred keeping cool with McFlurries...

CHAPTER 122

Thank you, Susan, for the lovely visit today and the Poodle Mountain plaque

All our little ones remembered

We'll be putting the Daisy one up near her "ruler of the universe" plot

CHAPTER 123

Good Morning from Poodle Central....

A little light tale today,

Lupin .... whose mission in life apparently is to turn me grey, has, since she arrived been fascinated by the 🛁 bath

She's jumped in, dragged the plug out and ran with it, ran with my towels like they are stuffies and generally had a good time

However, she's now giving the bath a wide berth...

Why??

Well, the other night I was running a bath and Lupin was hanging around (Teddy and Alfie were in the suitcase nest) and wham!!

In she jumps!

Well quicker than lightening I'm diving (I now know exactly what a swan dive looks like 😵) after her and grabs her as her feet hit the ankle deep (hot) water 💦

Lupin let's rip a *"Yip!"*

And I'm running with her handing her to Neil who promptly plopped her in the paddling pool

Thankfully no scolding

Just a now very wary Lupin ...eyes staring at the bath accusingly

As you can see, she was in full Lupin form yesterday playing ball and later lying with Teddy like a "broken" Lupini 😄

Quiet????...

I've heard of this ...what is it?

CHAPTER 124

Good Evening from Poodle Central.....

Lupin would like to show you her big sisters photo frames

Carol sent one when the Boo was taken from us and she has now sent one for Daisy

Both girls together and perfect on the fireplace

Samantha, Thank you for the card and the beautiful Daisy ring

The words are perfect
"I think of you every Daisy"

Lastly
Neil says Rachel
You're on his high-five list!

The get well soon card was unexpected and made him smile ☺xx

We are truly blessed

CHAPTER 125

I AM POODLE
HEAR ME ROAR!!!

CHAPTER 126

Soooo...

Daisy and Belle won't be with us to run on the beach 🏖️

But no Parkinson is ever left behind or forgotten

So, I've changed their photos in their frames to show them at the beach and they will come with us tomorrow 🖼️🖼️🖤

CHAPTER 127

First trip to the beach for the Lupini ....

And she thought the sand was snow 😕 she tried galloping through it

Teddy enjoyed himself with a mound of sand
And Alfie had a wander

Then on the way back Teddy decided he hurt his paw ...so I picked him up

Got to the car 🚗 and he was fine!

The little so and so just wanted a picky 😄

<u>CHAPTER 128</u>

Super Poodle walk today at Theddlethorpe

Ok, the heavens opened at one stage but we carried on!

The poodles tall and small had fun

The Lupini enjoyed her very first poodle walk and meeting new poodle friends 🐩🐩

Then back to Sandy's for yummy cake and snacks

CHAPTER 129

So....

We've been out walking today and Alfie and Teddy are knackered ...

The Lupini???

Oh no
She's currently playing ball with Neil

The England match means nothing to Lupin 😊😊

She'll have 30 mins nap time after this and then be back on full power 🐾

CHAPTER 130

So, as you can see the
gang were lazy lumps
this morning ......

Teddy says all this
"yomping" is no good for
him, he prefers a sedate
stroll, ambling along

Lupin says she likes the comfy bed
And Alfie says he's no idea where he's visited...

Anyways we took them back to the beach walk
from yesterday, this morning and got to the beach
where Teddy promptly sat down 🐾

He was going no further ...

So, Lupin and Alfie went
on the beach while I
carried (yes carried) the
tired little Tedster back to
the car for a nice rest

The moral???

It's no easy task carrying
a tired Teddy back to the
car- but as every good
poodle wrangler knows
needs must 🐾🖤

CHAPTER 131

Welcome to Pool gate...

I'm in the dog house with Miss Lupin ...

She is currently sat on the sofa in the caravan and giving me scowls if I happen to walk by ...

Why????? Come the cries!

Well, this morning their dad got a pool for them and blew it up 👍

I nipped into to Chapel St Leonard's and bought the gang a baby octopus 🐙each

Pink for Lupin
Blue and green for the boys
All is well

The weather is very very warm and both Teddy and Lupin were warm...

So, I had a bright idea 💡

I plopped Lupin in the pool and wet her, closely followed by a running away Teddy

Ta! Da! 2 cool poodles

Well, this is where it went wrong ☹

Lupin threw me the filthiest of looks and dropped her new octopus 🐙in the water and marched off!

Teddy was more forgiving

So now Lupin is sat indoors with Alfie telling her tale of woe- how her bad mum wet her through 💧💧💧💧💧

CHAPTER 132

Just sitting on the caravan deck with the Tedster

CHAPTER 133

Good Afternoon from Poodle Central......

Well, we haven't said those words for a while ....
but today we've been busy at Poodle Central,

Lupin's pool was seconded to the spongeathon
for the group and a few good sponges were
thrown at Neil

Alfie decided all this was just too much and
preferred to sit in the living room with his fan

Lupin sadly was in the wrong place at the right
time lol and got hosed by Auntie Sue, however she
minded not one jot as she got to share a butterfly
cake afterwards

And the Tedster??

Well as we know Teddy is allergic to water so
he kept a low profile whilst the sponges were
about

But now he's currently sitting next to Daisy's plot
- it's one of his favourite spots at the moment
Miss Lupin is flat out

And Alfie is very cool 😎

CHAPTER 134

Good Morning from Poodle Central....

Well, the Lupini rose at 3.30am ready to play 😬

A few words had the sulking Lupin scowling from a nest (and if she could) muttering "make hay while the sun shines"

Well 8am everyone woke and I knew today was going to be "one of those" when Alfie calmly strolled up to Lupin's pool and pee pee'd up the side with a horrified Lupin looking on 😱

Teddy? well the thinker of the family had decided snakey 🪨needed an outing and the little man dragged snakey and plopped him near Daisy

Now I'm sure Daisy would have had a few choice words about this snakey action, while Belle would be silently cursing

However, I'm sure the Tedster was giving a nod to both his sisters and that they are together

Teddy managed to get to his sofa before a pumped-up Lupin broke into wacky races around poodle mountain - mad as a bag of badgers 😆

Then went to get the ball out of the paddling pool All this before 9am....

Teddy and Alfie are currently snoozing on the sofa
And Lupin???

Well, looking
for mischief of
course 🙄😜😜

CHAPTER 135

Good Evening from Poodle Central......

Do things get quiet here?

No is the answer

It's Bo Bo time Alfie and Teddy are taking up their positions on the bed and enter stage left......

Lupin and Miss Snakey 🐍

The boys file a complaint, it's Bo Bo time
Lupin blows a raspberry 👅

I just think .... now what did I do with those earplugs?

CHAPTER 136

Good Afternoon from Poodle Central....

Well today it just shows you small doesn't mean un noticed...

I had to take Lupin to the vets as we thought she was having a pancreatic incident ....so armed with some pain relief and pro biotic paste, off we were a trotting ...ok me trotting Lupin scowling

As we were going out one of the receptionist's said Parkinson- I thought I recognised that name, Oh Mrs Parkinson I'm sorry I've not seen you but can I just say I'm so sorry about Daisy May

I turned Lupin still scowling at me

Thank you I said, thank you for remembering Daisy

Oh, she was beautiful she replied, there were a few tears shed that week when we all heard

Me ...... thank you 🖤

Off we went home

And so, my little ruler of the universe carries on, her impact made 🕯️🖤🎀

And the Lupini? well she's forgiven me ...I think 😊

CHAPTER 137

Good morning from Poodle Central......

Well, the horde ...oops I mean the little sweethearts ☺have been up and roaming about early today ...

I did ask for a lie in as I pulled my back the other day but apparently, I didn't file the right paperwork with them ☺

Teddy was up first, stretching his legs and strolling down stairs for his early morning pee pee, quickly followed by Lupin who is determined she won't miss anything (even a pee pee)

Well just as they arrived back in bed .... I heard the "clap clap" 👀

The rat (the neighbours Shih Tzu) had come out at the back of us and his "dad" (I'm using that term through gritted teeth) is now taking great pleasure in clapping their announcement ☺

Why???

To get Teddy and Lupin running outside to the rat run ☺

This was 7am
Me silently keeping my fingers and toes crossed that Teddy and Lupin don't hear the clapping ...

And??
No, they didn't hear, or more likely decided it was too early lol

Me shouting silently Yes!
All settles down
Feels movement on the bed and then something dropping on my head…

Squeezing my eyes shut
The item drops on my head again

Me one eye open and staring straight into the face of Lupin … who had now decided its play time and is dropping her tennis 🎾 ball on my head 🙄

It's Bo Bo time!
Lupin…. are you mad?? It's daylight and the suns shining

Me…. look Teddy and Alfie are sleeping

Lupin …not for long, over she trots to Tedd and gives him an unwelcome prod

Tedd gets up and marches off into his hole …

Lupin staring at me …
Fine!!! I'm awake

Throws ball
Off Lupin gallops, grabs the ball and…. flipping runs straight downstairs to play with her dad! 😀
😀

So now I'm awake and I've been duped by a poodle

Ah well cup of tea ☕ me thinks

CHAPTER 138

I'm back!!!!!!

CHAPTER 139

Now before any one says ....no Lupins were harmed in this "corning" 😋

Lupin is debating her next move...

I've got a bit of payback 🙄 after this morning's ball event

I wanted to put a 'corn' in her pom but she moved mid fastening and now is glaring at me 😀

I am fixing it ...
But sorry Lupin you've been papped! 😳😳😳

CHAPTER 140

Good Afternoon from Poodle Central....

It's a sad-happy day today

Miss Lupin has finally moved into a drawer of her own to store her jumpers and coats

And today we boxed up Daisy's and Belles coats and jumpers, my beautiful girls, always forever

In personalised boxes

CHAPTER 141

Good morning from Poodle central....

You've reached us in a tense standoff and the poodle horde - well Teddy and Lupin - have been running around like 2 mad goons

Why???

Well, the weather dry, the back doors open and the toys are outside ...

Ok you say, that's good

Yes, it's good but it also means it's like wacky races, even poor Alfie has put in a complaint about the noise!

Add that to the fact the neighbour's "rat" is out galloping too and there's no peace 😵

So that's when I put my foot down!

Lupin! Teddy!
In!
Shouts again
In!
In comes 2 muttering poodles

Right let's just play nicely for a while
Lupin 🐩

Teddy toddled off to his hole for a bit of hedgy time 🦔

Now Lupins idea of quiet?

Stood in my living room window sill shouting at 2 sparrows who happen to land in the garden

Lupin!
Shut your mouth!
Lupin - I'm on protection duty
Me- sparrows????

Lupin - running up and down the window sill
Ok ok I say that's it!

Out the window!
And this, my friends are where you join us
Me saying out
Lupin saying no

Well, she did come out - a treat can break many a resolve lol

Currently her and Teddy are back outside
Teddy looking for the rat

And Lupin? well she's deciding how to turn the paddling pool over (it's on its side and rain has filled it a little)

Thankfully Alfie is sitting nicely next to me - cup of tea time

CHAPTER 142

Good morning from Poodle Central....

You know it's not going to be a quiet day when Neil, Teddy and Lupin have all left for the park but you come downstairs and find snakey at the back door

I don't know whether he's trying to do a runner or he's been abandoned by a Lupini showing him the sights of the garden

Either way I'll finish my cup of tea and restore snakey to his hole before Teddy arrives back home

what he doesn't see and all that

CHAPTER 143

Good Evening from Poodle Central....

You find us just having finished wacky races....

Everyone had settled down to watch some TV, however the Lupini could be heard upstairs galloping around....

Teddy did go and investigate, however all Snakeys were present so he came back downstairs and flopped next to Alfie

Watching TV 📺

And Bamm!
Lupin running .... with my new reef flip flop in her mouth! 😱

Me- Lupin!

Lupin- anything on the floor is mine! mine I tell Ya!
And I'm up and running!

Lupins running up the stairs
I'm a running behind

She runs around the bed, I'm after her!

But she throws me a blinder! she jumps on the bed flip flop tucked between her gnashers!

Lupin!

She turns.... drops the flip flop 🩴 and I swear she laughs before grabbing the flip flop and galloping down the stairs

I'm a running
And......

There she is sat next to her
dad - butter wouldn't melt in
her mouth

Flip flop abandoned at the
bottom of the stairs!
Me muttering

Lupin - same time tomorrow?

CHAPTER 144

Good Afternoon from Poodle Central!!!

Breaking news!!!

Randy has been finally located after the hedgehog mafia Hoo Har and someone's had a "go" at his leg!

Randy was found at the Stuffie emergency window sill shortly after lunchtime holding onto his gammy leg

He remains tight lipped about what happened but speculation is rife!!

He's currently undergoing surgery to sew his leg back on and the prognosis is good by his doctor AKA me 😬

Unless Randy talks or squawks then the culprit will get away....

CHAPTER 145

Good Afternoon from Poodle Central......

We bring you live from the scene of an amazing heist!

And the booty.... Randy Rooster!!!

All was going well this morning, the hedgehog mafia was quietly conversing with Randy and they had even gone outside to take in some sun

However, things took an unexpected turn and bamm! - The hedgehogs grabbed Randy and started running across the lawn!!

Lupin gave chase!

Trying valiantly to save Randy, who was being bobbed up and down like a rooster rotisserie

In the end she shouted for assistance and Teddy and Alfie came a running Teddy tried to reason with his rogue hedgies

but no, they were on a mission
And so, the Hedgehog mafia .... gulp...has Randy!!!

CHAPTER 146

Good Morning from Poodle Central!

Amazing news!

There has been an early morning rescue of Randy Rooster! (Who was a bit worse for wear as it seems he's been partying 🍗🍗 with his captives the hedgehog 🦔mafia)

A meeting was seen being assembled involving Lupin, Teddy, Alfie and Miss Snakey!

Shortly thereafter a howl was heard at camp hedgehog and Randy was seen galloping - er slithering away on Miss Snakey!

Lupin was quoted as saying "I love it when a plan comes together"

Randy said he needed a drink 🥃

Teddy and Alfie were seen searching for the hedgehog 🦔mafia

CHAPTER 147

Good Morning from Poodle Central......

A different tale this morning ...

Lupin was sat next to me while I was having my cup of tea

I look at her and say all her sisters and brothers will be watching her

Lupin 🐾

Yes, I say, do you know each and every one of them arrived here at Poodle Central exactly when they were meant to

Lupin watching me

I then told her the tale of when her sister Belle arrived one Saturday afternoon - you see Lupin, Belle 's first family was just a stop gap until it was time for her to come here

Lupin eyes wide

That's what rescues do I said, they take all the poodles and then place them exactly where they should be

Belle was brought by 2 special people and look she grew up to be a world famous snakeynapper

Lupin looking at me and glances at her now mangled lamb chop stuffy

Don't worry I say destuffing stuffies is an art 🙄

Lupin looks back at me

So, you see I tell her, if and maybe when Daisy decides to send anyone our way, we'll know they are arriving at exactly the right time and to exactly the right place

Lupin...you mean you knew I was coming???

Oh yes, I say it took you a while to get here, and you had adventures along the way

but yes you too Lupin arrived exactly when you should of

And the moral???

Yes, it is perfectly reasonable to have an in-depth conversation with your poodle

Providing your poodle wants to listen 🐾🐾🐾🖤

<u>CHAPTER 148</u>

Good Evening from Poodle Central....

Alfie had his vet check appointment today and sadly he's got a deteriorated collapsed trachea

He already has an epiglottis flap issue 😿

He's back next week for more tests and x-rays

In the meanwhile, he's some meds for inflammation

Then we consider if he is a surgery candidate ...
But as usual at Poodle Central we move forward; we will get the best treatment and care Alfie deserves

CHAPTER 149

Good Evening from Poodle Central....

Well, the Tedster thought Alfie needed some sea air...

So, he messaged our good friends Jacqueline and Olga and Ta! Da!

The Parkinson's are going to Wales and beach running pretty soon

Big Thanks to Jacqueline and Olga, Pronto and Eimear 🖤🖤

CHAPTER 150

Good Morning from Poodle Central....

Ok maybe I didn't think through putting the groups Grab a Ducks in Lupins pool......😟😟

As this morning out shoot the little darlings and "Stop!" Lupin put her brakes on ....

She stops
She looks
She looks at me 🔲
I see a glint...

And there you go!. Lupin's head is in the pool trying to play "Grab a Duck!"

Lupin!!

Leave those ducks alone! No grabbing today!

Yes, I did actually shout that 😃

Lupin? If I grab it, it's mine!

Teddy strolls past Lupin now balanced on the inflatable side of the pool...

I see him lift his eyebrows

Now this is where Lupin should have been watching...

I'm inside, one eye on Lupin making sure all the ducks are safe

And Alfie ambles by after finishing his morning pee pee...

You know where I going don't you?

Picture a balanced Lupin
A blind Alfie making his way to the door

And ....
Bam!!

Alfie accidentally knocks against Lupin's pool,

dislodges the balanced Lupin and splash! a now damp Lupin!

Well, she was out of that pool like the clappers!
Ducks forgotten

Teddy and Alfie sat on sofa

And a damp pommed Lupin sitting glaring in the window

Ah well....

At least it will be quiet while I have my cup of tea

CHAPTER 151

Good Evening from Poodle Central...

I'll leave you with this tonight...

All the ducks are safe! However, I had to remove them from Lupins paddling pool 😕

As she had grabbed one and threw it under the TV unit 😵

Here is Miss Lupin still trying to "Grab a Duck" 😀

<u>CHAPTER 152</u>

Good Evening from Poodle Central....

Mr Alf is currently side-lined and receiving medical care so all is very quiet at PC

Lupin is recharging her batteries (I see a 3am playtime on the horizon)

The Tedster is thinking ....

But he makes himself comfortable 😕 he's running a take on the princess and the pea 😃

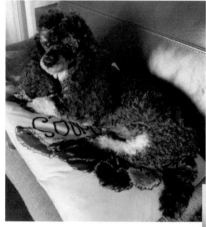

CHAPTER 153

Good Morning from Poodle Central....

You know I can remember the day when every single bundle arrived here,

Either when we went on a road trip to collect them or when they knocked at our front door – I remember the smiles, the joy and the love ....

Now as everyone knows I always say age is not an illness, and God love her my Daisy ruler of the universe proved that time and time again...

However, the one thing we cannot protect them from is time ...Time is the cruellest adversary of them all

Alfie will be having his X-rays and Scans today but when the vets telephoned early this morning, they also said in their opinion Alfie has canine cognitive dysfunction or doggy dementia at an advanced level

Have we not noticed it? - I say yes we've seen his little blips but we work round them and adapt to Alfie - it's all about Alfie being happy

Fate is being particularly cruel to us at the moment, but I must also flip that by saying although we've suffered some losses we've been blessed by the wonderful Boo and her ability to surpass any medical expectations of her - we've been graced by Daisy ruler of the universe - So, we are incredibly lucky
Please if you can, spare a kind thought for "Alf Malf" today - We shall aim to win a battle at a time

CHAPTER 154

An update on Alfie ...

The vets have reported back
Alfie's trachea is not in as bad shape as predicted
- it looks ok

However, he has chronic bronchitis or COPD this
will be adding to his coughing

There is some mucus/fluid
He has 2 benign masses on his spleen
He has a 2cm mass on his liver but they cannot
confirm it's benign (yet)

However, the big find was
Alfie's tummy was full to burst
with food

This will have been making
him very uncomfortable and
sick - They are giving him
meds to get rid of the food and
will rescan him tomorrow

Some of his organs are
inflamed around his tummy
but this could be due to his
tummy taking up a lot of room

We are concentrating on the
tummy issue - He is on the meds
He is staying in hospital

We will visit him later

This was Alfie going to the vets yesterday and you
can see he looked very worried/unhappy

CHAPTER 155

Thank you everyone for the "Poodle Army's" support re our Alf Malf

The vets have called this morning and Alfie is comfortable

However, they have put a feeding tube in through his nose as he won't take any food off them

So, this way he's getting little bits

They are rescanning today to check his tummy and organs

Alfie has poodle central genes running through him and he's a tough cookie

I'm just glad he's more settled and comfortable Lupin has been told to comfort the Tedster today as he's very quiet

As everyone knows he's the family's thinker and at present I can see the little "wheels" running in Tedd's mind - "Alfie's gone to the vets but he hasn't come back"

Teddy was so disappointed last night when we didn't come back with Alfie

<u>*CHAPTER 156*</u>

Extra good thoughts needed for Alfie!

The vets have telephoned and Alfie's tummy is not clearing,

They have tried meds

They have tried extra meds

So, the vet has now asked for permission to give Alfie anaesthetic and pump his stomach to get rid of the glup

This is the least invasive

We need his tummy to clear

I love you Alf Malf 🖤

CHAPTER 157

Many ...ok many many years ago when I got my first poodle, an unsaid oath was born

To stand in front of them and protect

Over the years this has brought me smiles and broke my heart ......

This time last year at Poodle Central we were a family of 6 and the first whisperings of Christmas were being uttered

However, no one ever said poodle wrangling was easy, you always need one eye on the horizon

Our little family has been shattered by loss and excited by a new arrival

Today we find ourselves waiting ...and I will say it.... praying

I've spoken to Alfie's vet this morning and they are very concerned

Alfie is not eating (well he's not going to with a full tummy)

He's not pooping, and he was very restless last night

The vets are concerned that all scans show the food in Alfie's tummy acting as normal, but it's not clearing

They now think blockage
And a grizzly blockage

The vet threw it into the pot, is it worth emptying Alfie's tummy? if something is then found?

After all he's 14

Well, I kindly told her the same as I always do

age is not an illness and unless we empty Alfie's tummy then we cannot move forward

Alfie will get the best care and if something is found then we will cross that bridge when we get there
Ok she says

Then started to tell me the costs, I'll stop you there I said - all that matters is Alfie, costs do not

So today they are going to perform the stomach pump and give Alfie much needed relief, then rescan and a CT scan

As I write this, I must admit I'm a little numb, I thought our horrendous times were over and fate was allowing us to just enjoy, however I shall have a cup of tea and stand up tall and do as I said when Alfie came through our door all those years ago

I will stand in front of you and protect

CHAPTER 158

Alfie update ......

I've spoken to the vets and Alfie's got over the first hurdle ....

They've pumped his stomach which was full of green gunky liquid

The scan showed the stomach was empty of the gunk
Alfie is comfortable

Tonight, they are going to feed Alfie little amounts to see if the stomach processes the food as it should

He will be rescanned tomorrow

So, fingers crossed everyone 🤞🤞🤞🤞🤞🤞

My poor little man, he's being pulled through the ringer

CHAPTER 159

Good morning from Poodle Central......

We still await further news on Alfie

But in the meantime, Miss Lupin or the (rolls eyes) amazing Lupini as she would like to be known 😕 has been trying to keep everyone's spirits up

So may I present...

Lupin gets her ducks in a row
Lupin shows the ducks who's boss
Well, it can only be best described as "the mad Lupini!"

Teddy just rolled his eyes
Enjoy!

We at poodle central await news on tender hooks

CHAPTER 160

Alfie update......

Overnight Alfie was given little amounts of food

He was scanned early this morning and his tummy is not processing the food 😔

His tummy is filling up again

Our options were very limited, as Alfie's tummy is refilling, so unless we want to do another pump (which we don't) we have to act fast

So please send the most positive vibes to our little man

This afternoon Alfie is going to surgery and being opened up in the hope the vets can see what the problem is

We tried to get a camera procedure but this couldn't be done until late next week and time is of the essence

The vets will telephone us with an update later

CHAPTER 161

Update on Alfie

The vets opened Alfie up and finally they could see Alfie's problem

The pyloric tube - the bottom tube allowing food out of the tummy - has narrowed

This they believe is due to muscle thickening - they can feel no masses

So, the head surgeon has come in and they are performing a pyloric stent

And confirming no masses inside the tube

The vet we spoke to had no idea of the length of surgery but she said they would ring later this evening

Hopefully this will now let Alfie tummy process the food

Thank you everyone for the continued support for our little Alf x

CHAPTER 162

Update on Alfie ....

The vets have telephoned ....

The surgery went well and the stent is in

Alfie is currently receiving additional oxygen as his levels were low

The vet said, she's glad we went for surgery as Alfie needed it

She also said she thought we were brave to "go for it" considering Alfie's condition and age but it was the right decision

I told her not brave

We always said Alfie had to have the best chance and we would follow through however difficult

So now this last hurdle is to be overcome, let's get Alfie over the surgery and his levels back to normal

<u>CHAPTER 163</u>

Update on Alf Malf....

Alfie is now off the oxygen and very settled
No pacing in his kennel

They have fed him through the feeding tube and
this afternoon they are rescanning him to make
sure his tummy is passing food

He's been through the wars and beat every battle

The operation has been done so let's 👍👍👍to a
good scan this afternoon

CHAPTER 164

A week ago tomorrow we took Alfie to the vets as he'd been very unsettled Saturday night

It's been a roller coaster week

Tests, tests and more tests

Unplanned exploratory surgery followed by surgery to place a stent

Scan upon scan

Well today Alfie's tummy is finally doing what it should!

It's been scanned and it's passing food normally

The only blip is he's a little compacted in his colon so a mild laxative will help

But all being well the vets are discharging Alfie tomorrow!!!

Admittedly with his feeding tube - but hopefully we'll kick that to the curb soon

I can't thank everyone enough for all your kind thoughts, healing words and prayers at our lowest ebb

I'm sorry if I've not replied to each and every one but your support has meant so much

CHAPTER 165

Lupin V the duck squad

Duckies -0
Lupin – 10

And as a side scrag,

Lupin V Miss Snakey

Miss Snakey - missing end of her tail
Lupin - very pleased with herself

CHAPTER 166

Update on Alfie....

Well, we brought the Alfmyster home and yes, he looked like he'd been dragged through a hedge backwards

I see the vet's creative groomer has been in the house 🙄 and Alfie is now sporting 2 poms

We've been a little late doing the update as Alfie was quite restless last night - he couldn't settle and had the sensation to pee pee but wasn't "going"

Also, he'd developed a limp?

The feeding tube went ok

This morning he's had a good hour or so flat out and had some solid foods (admittedly only a small amount) but he wants the solids so that is good

He's still got a limp at the front

And we've still got the pee pee problem

I've spoken to the vets who have said to monitor and if we feel anything gets worse to bring him back in otherwise, they will see us tomorrow at 2pm

CHAPTER 167

Alfie's had his feeding tube removed!!

The vets were super pleased with him!

His stitches on his tummy are dissolvable
I've not got a photo of him yet "tubeless"

But here's Alfie and Lupin earlier this morning
Alfie had 2 problems with this photo –

1. He's now got "Lupin poms!"

2. Lupin stands to attention and made Alfie look
teeny (Lupin isn't that much bigger than Alfie lol)

CHAPTER 168

Calling on the Poodle Army!!

Alfie took his beloved gnome in hospital last week and the vets "appear" to have lost it 😦

I can say some choice words from me were uttered

I can assure you I stressed the point that they better find the gnome as it's Alfie's number one stuffy

His Auntie Ruth bought it him one Christmas

Please if anyone knows where these gnomes are for sale - let me know! (it's the little gnome on the left second photo)

Here's a photo of Alfie with his gnome for reference

CHAPTER 169

Good Afternoon from Poodle Central......

It's gnometopia here!

I went to B&M this morning but sadly came away empty handed ....

However, my apologies to Alf we're short lived...a knock a knock at the door ...

And a package arrived...
A gnome!!!

I immediately presented green gnome to Alf and I have to say I smiled when Alf smelled the gnome and then dragged a foot under him

Later snuggling up with his new gnome

However, that wasn't the end of Alfie's new gnomes... another delivery

And another gnome came a calling ....

Alfie is feeling rather loved up at the moment after nearly a week without his beloved gnome

Big thank you goes out to Alfie's gnome god mother Karen

You really have made a little man's day

Teddy???...not interested unless it's a hedgy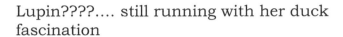

Lupin????.... still running with her duck
fascination

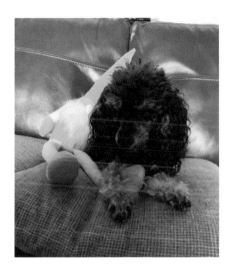

CHAPTER 170

Poodle Central has relocated (well for this week 😜)

We're on tour at
Porthcawl!

Gnomes✔
Snakeys ✔
Ducks ✔
Hedgehogs ✔

Tomorrow we visit a
beach and castle 🏰

CHAPTER 171

Today's castle ....

A trip to Ogmore
Castle
Lupin met some sheep
😐
Lupin shouting at the
horses
Teddy found a magic
stone
And Ta! Da!

The castle has "stepping stones" across the river
Ewenny these have been there since "forever"

Many tourists try their luck across the stones
We saw a lady fall in today 😨

So, like any good Poodle Wrangler I grabbed my 2
trusty assistants and set off galloping over the
stones!

Neil took the photos of us
going across and coming
back!
Yep!
We made it in one piece

(Well, I did promise Teddy)

CHAPTER 172

Good Afternoon from Poodle Central on tour in Wales......

We didn't go far today as Alfie wasn't feeling well, so it's the Dragon Trail...

Sssh...dragon prints!

And a very attractive stream - if you're a Lupin 😀 😀

Lastly - Ta! Da!
Our own piece of Welsh driftwood for our garden!

CHAPTER 173

Poodle Central is back in Bolton!

Que a sulking Teddy who absolutely loves caravan life...

Lupin knew the party was over when we took her harness off

And Alfie???.... well, he's living the dream....
another gnome greeted him when he arrived home
(please tell me if you sent it, as there's no note)

Big thanks to our super friends Jacqueline and Olga and Pronto and Eimear for allowing us to spend time in your beautiful caravan

Teddy says he (we) will be back next year

CHAPTER 174

Good Evening from Poodle Central....

It's been bath day here and it's a title I'm sure she didn't want but

Dirtiest Little Parkinson goes to ......

Lupini!

Yep, as you can see her bath water was quite literally mucky

Both Alfie and Teddy were mucky pups too, but not it seems as much as chief muckmyster Lupin

CHAPTER 175

Ok Lupin…
Start explaining…

How a dolphin has landed slap in the middle of
your duckies 😟😟

<u>*CHAPTER 176*</u>

Good Afternoon from Poodle Central......

Good grief! I turn my back and wham!

Now even I can't make out this pow wow and what's happening 😶😶

But it appears Miss Snakey has found a few friends and is in talks with the duckies!

Now the questions here are

where is snakey??? 🐿
Is this anything to do with the hedgehog 🦔mafia???

Where are Alfie and Teddy???
And what the heck is Lupin doing sat in the middle of this pow wow????

I sit sipping my cup of tea ☕watching this....and thinking maybe I best have a glass of wine later 😀

CHAPTER 177

Good Afternoon from Poodle Central....

Well, we left things in a whole to do yesterday....

2 missing duckies...
A meeting of the Snakeys led by Miss Snakey and the Duckies....

So many questions???

And Lupin sat right there in the middle!!

Now investigations continued yesterday and this morning - no stone was left unturned ...

Teddy's hole was searched - he's filed a formal complaint

Still no sign of the missing duckies ....
Lupin was keeping tight lipped

Alfie thought everywhere he was standing there was a Stuffie!

Teddy remained calm and watched these proceedings
I'd thought the duckies were lost!

Until when I came downstairs there was a commotion .... ahh the "rat" is out I thought

No!!
The mystery was solved!

The lord of lush himself turned up! those 2 impressionable duckies had been partying with Randy!!!

Ycs, it started yesterday and gnomes were involved 😜

but when the gnomes passed out Randy and the 2 duckies carried on partying and passed out under the TV cabinet!!

So, you'd think today would be a quiet day??

No Randy was re charged and declared it party time in the back garden!

And anyone who's who attended....

The Snakeys including Snakey 🐍!

All the duckies
The gnomes
And even the hedgehog 🦔mafia!

Randy is currently nursing a sore head but I'm pleased to report all stuffies are present and correct

Teddy watched all this from his bench in the garden...watching, thinking

Alfie wondered where the heck his gnomes had gone???

And Hmmmmm Lupin??.... well yet again I'm the midst of things 😩😩😩

What does Lupin know??

Did the Lupini know where Randy and her 2 lost duckies were all along??

Is there someone pulling Lupini's strings? Or is she just in the right place at the right time???

CHAPTER 178

The Lupini is knackered!
Mum - 1

CHAPTER 179

Good Evening from Poodle Central......

Now c'mon hold your hand up if you can truly say you've said this when you go up to bed......

Is that a snakey that's been dragged out from under the bed

😀😀😀😀
No????

Darn just me then

And with that my friends we've reached the end of the tales from Poodle Central for now.

I hope you will join us again soon and we can laugh and share the wonderful world of Poodles

Until then keep an eye on the hedgehogs you never know what they are up to.

Facebook Group: We're all about Poodles.

Printed in Poland
by Amazon Fulfillment
Poland Sp. z o.o., Wrocław
12 October 2022

f717d613-d503-4ac8-b78b-dfc1629555beR01